Why There's ANTIFREEZE in Your TOOTHPASTE

The Chemistry of Household Ingredients

SIMON QUELLEN FIELD

CHICAGO REVIEW PRESS

Library of Congress Cataloging-in-Publication Data
Field, Simon (Simon Quellen)
    Why there's antifreeze in your toothpaste : the
chemistry of household ingredients / Simon Quellen
Field. — 1st ed.
        p. cm.
Includes index.
ISBN-13: 978-1-55652-697-8
ISBN-10: 1-55652-697-0
    1. Chemicals.   2. Chemical elements.   3. Organic
compounds.   4. Inorganic compounds.   I. Title.

QD471.F565 2007
540—dc22

                                        2007025849

Cover photo: Mark Harwood/Stone Images
Cover and interior design: Scott Rattray
Structural illustrations: Michael Rattray

Published by Chicago Review Press, Incorporated
814 North Franklin Street
Chicago, Illinois 60610
ISBN-13: 978-1-55652-697-8
ISBN-10: 1-55652-697-0
Printed in the United States of America
5   4   3   2   1

Contents

Introduction

This book started in my shower.

The label on my shampoo bottle listed many compounds, and, due to my interest in chemistry, most of them were familiar or had obvious functions. However, one compound stood out as puzzling: sodium chloride.

Why was there salt in my shampoo?

Since I wasn't likely to be eating it, I doubted it was for seasoning, despite the strawberry aroma of the liquid. It could have been used as a preservative, but the remaining ingredients were more likely to kill microbes than salt was.

Once dry and dressed, I was still curious, so I wrote a letter to the manufacturer asking why there was salt in my shampoo. I received a surprisingly enlightening response from the company. Someone there had actually discussed the issue with a chemist and sent back to me an answer that made sense.

The ingredients in the shampoo come from many different manufacturers, in many different places around the world. From day to day, a particular batch of shampoo may differ significantly from the previous day's batch in the amount of moisture brought in with those ingredients. Salt has the effect of thickening the mixture, and is added to each batch in the amount needed to raise the viscosity to a specified level. Consequently, the customer gets a product that pours the same way each time. This consistency is important to the customer, because a watery product can cause suspicions about value or about possible tampering.

I have told this story many times when teaching chemistry to popular audiences. There are thousands of chemical compounds in the ingredients lists of products we use every day. If you're comparison shopping, knowing what each compound is doing in the product has obvious benefits. However, it also provides a sneaky way of teaching simple chemistry to people who had no idea they would find it so interesting and who see chemistry simply as the domain of nerds with masking tape on their eyeglasses.

Sprinkled throughout this book are sidebars focusing on foods and consumer products that use interesting ingredients; the sidebars explain just what those ingredients are doing in those particular products.

The bulk of the book is a more in-depth discussion of each compound, usually accompanied by a structural formula, a picture of the chemical that allows it to be compared to others. It is in these sections that you will occasionally find clearly marked "Chemistry Lessons." If I have done my job properly, these will be interesting, and they'll relate to the compound that caught your interest in the first place.

This book can act as a reference. You can use the index to look up an ingredient you find on a label and find out more about it. It may point you to other pages or other compounds; you may enjoy reading the book in this random fashion, rather than from front to back. Feel free to do so. Feel free to skip over sections that don't relate to what you are trying to find out. The book will still be there later when you have another question.

This book is not about scaring people. So much of the information out there about additives or chemicals in common products is written to alarm people into changing their behavior in ways that potentially enrich the writer. They point to the MSDS for a compound—the Material Safety Data Sheets—that list all the dire consequences and safety precautions associated with a compound.

An MSDS can be quite frightening. Here is an excerpt from a typical MSDS:

Hazards Identification

WARNING! CAUSES EYE IRRITATION.

Lab Protective Equip: GOGGLES; LAB COAT

May cause mild irritation to the respiratory tract.

Very large doses can cause vomiting, diarrhea, and prostration. Dehydration and congestion occur in most internal organs. Hypertonic solutions can produce violent inflammatory reactions in the gastrointestinal tract.

May irritate damaged skin; absorption can occur with effects similar to those via ingestion.

Causes irritation, redness, and pain.

First Aid Measures

Remove to fresh air. Get medical attention for any breathing difficulty.

If large amounts were swallowed, give water to drink and get medical advice.

Wash exposed area with soap and water. Get medical advice if irritation develops.

Immediately flush eyes with plenty of water for at least 15 minutes, lifting upper and lower eyelids occasionally. Get medical attention if irritation persists.

In the event of a fire, wear full protective clothing and NIOSH-approved self-contained breathing apparatus with full facepiece operated in the pressure demand or other positive pressure mode.

Ventilate area of leak or spill. Wear appropriate personal protective equipment.

Keep in a tightly closed container, stored in a cool, dry, ventilated area. Protect against physical damage. Containers of this material may be hazardous when empty since they retain product residues (dust, solids); observe all warnings and precautions listed for the product.

Wear protective gloves and clean body-covering clothing.

Use chemical safety goggles. Maintain eye wash fountain and quick-drench facilities in work area.

When heated to above 801°C (1474°F) it emits toxic fumes of chloride and sodium oxide.

Oral rat LD50: 3000 mg/kg.
Inhalation rat LD50: > 42 gm/m³ /1H.
Skin rabbit LD50: > 10 gm/kg. Investigated as a mutagen, reproductive effector.

Label Hazard Warning:
WARNING! CAUSES EYE IRRITATION.
Label Precautions:
Avoid contact with eyes.
Wash thoroughly after handling.
Label First Aid:
In case of eye contact, immediately flush eyes with plenty of water for at least 15 minutes. Get medical attention if irritation develops or persists.
Product Use:
Laboratory Reagent.

After reading that, you might expect that such a dangerous chemical had no business being around people, especially children. Yet in actuality, it's a chemical we can't live without: salt. And it's safe enough to put in shampoo.

What this illustrates is that an MSDS describes the dangers of large industrial quantities of a substance, not the tiny amounts usually found in consumer products. Nonetheless, once you are experienced at reading an MSDS, it is a good place to get information on the safety of a chemical compound. In this book I cover safety issues only occasionally—and briefly. To do a more thorough job of that would require a much larger book, and there is already a wealth of information available.

One should be wary, however, of authors who advise against a brand of toothpaste because "it has antifreeze in it!" Just before the publication of this book, a media frenzy arose over the discovery that a Chinese-made toothpaste contained the toxic additive diethylene glycol, which the Food and Drug Administration had warned had a "low but meaningful risk of toxicity and injury" to people with liver disease, people with kidney disease, and children. It was a poisoning incident involving diethylene glycol in 1937 that gave new regulatory powers to the FDA. And diethylene glycol makes a pretty good antifreeze.

But diethylene glycol is not glycerin or propylene glycol, both of which are nontoxic toothpaste ingredients that also have antifreeze properties, in addition to the emulsifying and moisturizing properties that are useful in toothpastes, cosmetics, baby wipes, bubble baths, medicines, flavorings, and shampoos.

So when someone warns that there is antifreeze in your toothpaste, ask which antifreeze. Some are illegal adulterants added by criminal cost-cutters, and their products are quickly recalled. Others (like glycerin, propylene glycol, or salt) are "generally recognized as safe" and are reasonable household ingredients.

Fear may help other folks to sell books or newspapers or organic toothpaste. But I hope *curiosity* is the reason you are reading my book.

How to Read Structural Formulas

Throughout this book, the description of each ingredient will include its chemical formula. This is often quite useful in comparing the ingredient to others, understanding how it performs its function, and evaluating how it interacts with other compounds.

Some of the formulas might look intimidating at first, but you can actually learn to read them in a few minutes, as the following text will show.

Simple Formulas

Some formulas, such as the formula for table salt, are very simple. You don't need a picture, just a description of the two elements that make it up: sodium and chlorine. The formula is:

$$NaCl$$

Other compounds are also fairly simple, although they may contain more elements. For example, phosphoric acid, a common ingredient used to provide tartness in soft drinks, is:

$$H_3PO_4$$

This formula says it is made up of three hydrogen atoms, one atom of phosphorus, and four atoms of oxygen.

A molecule you probably already know is water:

$$H_2O$$

Full Structural Formulas

For some compounds, it is especially useful to know the *shape* of the molecule. While this is critically important in large molecules made with a backbone of carbon, called organic molecules, it is often interesting in simpler molecules as well. The formula for water might cause you to think that a hydrogen atom was attached to another hydrogen atom, and then an oxygen atom was attached to them:

$$H - H - O$$

That would be wrong, however, since a hydrogen atom can only form a bond with one other atom. Moreover, oxygen can bond with two other atoms, so a better picture would look like this:

$$H - O - H$$

As it turns out, however, the angle between the bonds is not 180 degrees, as that picture would make it seem, but 105 degrees. This fact is important in understanding some curious facts about water:

The electrons that the hydrogen atoms share with the oxygen are located between the hydrogen atoms and the oxygen atom. This leaves the hydrogen atoms with a little bit of a positive charge, and the oxygen atom with a little bit of a negative charge. This *polar* arrangement means that the molecules prefer to align in certain ways, because the positive sides attract the negative sides. This gives water its surface tension. It explains why ice crystals arrange in hexagons and take up more space than liquid water, making ice less dense than water, so it floats. It also explains how water molecules can dissolve other polar molecules, such as table salt. The water molecules surround the positive sodium ions and the negative chlorine ions, and prevent them from getting back together.

Simplified Structural Formulas

I have already said that a hydrogen atom can only bond with one other atom. This is because it only has one electron to share. The element carbon has four electrons it can share easily, and so it can bond to four different atoms at a time. Because carbon is so versatile, it can form very complex molecules. These complex molecules are what led to life on this planet; living things are primarily made of large molecules with a backbone of carbon.

Simple carbon compounds such as methane are often written using nonstructural formulas, such as:

$$CH_4$$

or the structural formulas just discussed:

$$H - \underset{\underset{H}{|}}{\overset{\overset{H}{|}}{C}} - H$$

But when the molecules start getting larger, all those letters for carbon and hydrogen start to clutter up the page, making it hard to see detail.

Since carbon has four bonds to fill, and because hydrogen is the most likely atom to be attached to carbon in an organic molecule, chemists invented a shorthand notation that is easier to read and draw.

In this shorthand, they assume that any vertex between two lines contains a carbon atom unless specified otherwise. If there are several carbons in a row, they will make the lines join at angles, so that they can count the carbons if need be.

Chemists also say that any carbon that has fewer than four lines from it is assumed to have a hydrogen atom filling all the remaining bonds. Thus the molecule propane (C_3H_8), which has three carbons in a row, has all of the remaining bonds filled with hydrogen:

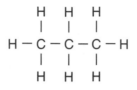

and becomes the much simpler looking picture:

There is a carbon at each end and one in the middle. The carbon atoms at each end have three remaining bonds, which are filled with three hydrogen atoms. The carbon in the middle has only two bonds left, so there are two hydrogen atoms there.

Now, for simple molecules like propane, this is not much of an improvement. It is easier to draw, but the reader has to do some thinking to figure out what the molecule is. However, with larger molecules, the simplification really helps to keep the picture uncluttered. Consider the molecule for aspartame, which would look like this:

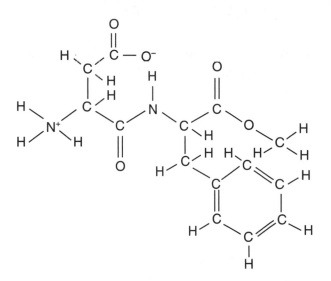

It simplifies to this:

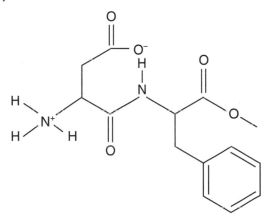

Three-Dimensional Structural Formulas

Sometimes it is important to know the three-dimensional structure of a molecule. In glucose, for example,

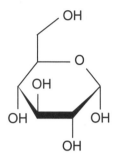

it is important to know which side of the molecule the various hydroxyl groups (the OH subunits) are on. Flipping one of them from the bottom to the top changes the sugar from glucose to galactose:

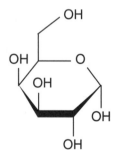

which is much less sweet than glucose.

The formula shown uses darker lines to indicate that some parts of the molecule are closer to the reader.

Preservatives

Preservatives have become the favorite target of people who want you to fear your food. Most preservatives are things you would not want to eat. Most preservatives taste bad and are toxic in large quantities, so it is not surprising that they have a bad reputation.

Preservatives generally fall into four categories. There are ultraviolet/UV light absorbers (to prevent light from creating harmful and bad-tasting toxins), color stabilizers, antioxidants, and antimicrobials.

One excellent UV protector for foods is PABA, a B vitamin. Likewise, many of the same antioxidants we ingest as health supplements—such as vitamin C and a similar chemical, erythorbic acid; vitamin E; and lecithin, a source of the important nutrients choline and inositol—occur naturally in food.

Some simple foods can be preservatives in their own right. Honey, salt, sugar, lactic acid, and vinegar are all examples of foods that inhibit microbial action. Some health professionals recommend consuming phytoestrogens from foods such as soybeans to achieve various health benefits. The phytoestrogens in the paraben family, found in blueberries, kill molds and fungi and are often added to food as preservatives.

But you don't have to choose between having sodium benzoate or *E. coli* bacteria in your soda. Bacteria can be controlled through pasteurization, a process that is used for milk but for some reason not for soft drinks.

Ultraviolet Light Absorbers

Benzophenone

Chemical Formula
$C_6H_5-C(O)-C_6H_5$

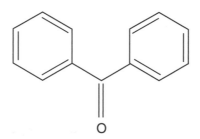

Synonyms
Diphenyl ketone • benzoyl benzene • phenyl ketone • diphenyl-methanone • alpha-oxodiphenylmethane • alpha-oxoditane

Description
White crystals with a rose- or geranium-like odor.

Uses
Benzophenone is used to prevent ultraviolet light from damaging scents and colors in products such as perfumes and soaps. It allows the manufacturer to package the product in clear glass or plastic. Without it, opaque or dark packaging would be necessary.

It can also be added to the plastic packaging itself as a UV blocker.

Benzophenone is also sometimes used as a flavoring agent.

Ultraviolet light is often divided into two types, UV-A, which has a longer wavelength (320–360 nm) and UV-B, which has a shorter wavelength (280–320 nm). Shorter wavelengths are higher energy wavelengths. UV-B is more damaging than UV-A. Some UV blockers are optimized to block the shorter wavelengths while letting the longer wavelengths get through.

Variants

There are many variants of benzophenone. They often have numbers after the name, a type of shorthand to indicate which variant is in use. The variations change features, such as solubility or the ease and functionality of bonding with plastics used in packaging. For example, benzophenone-2 is used in alcohol-based products, while benzophenone-5 is used in water-based products. Benzophenone-6 is used in nail polish, and benzophenone-9 is used in bath and skin-care products.

Some examples are shown below.

Benzophenone-3 (2-hydroxy-4-methoxybenzophenone)

Chemical Formula
$HOC_6H_3(OCH_3)COC_6H_5$

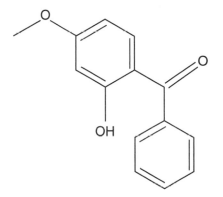

Benzophenone-3 can be added to plastic packaging as a UV blocker.

Benzophenone-4 (2-benzoyl-5-methoxy-1-phenol-4-sulfonic acid)

Chemical Formula
$C_{14}H_{12}O_6S$

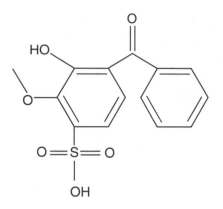

Benzophenone-4 is a water-soluble form used in cosmetics, hair-sprays, and hair dyes.

Benzophenone-bx-ahbp (4-allyloxy-2-hydroxy benzophenone)

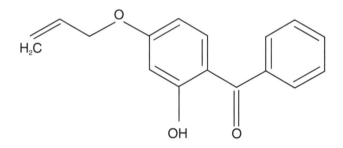

This form of benzophenone is also added to plastic packaging as a UV blocker. It bonds with the plastic and will not migrate out.

Other Examples

Benzophenone-1 (2,4-dihydroxy benzophenone)

Benzophenone-2 (2,2′,4,4′-tetrahydroxy benzophenone)

Benzophenone-5 (2-hydroxy-4-methoxy-5-sulfonyl benzophenone sodium salt)

Benzophenone-6 (2,2'-dihydroxy-4,4'-dimethoxy benzophenone)

Benzophenone-9 (2,2'-dihydroxy-4,4'-dimethoxy benzophenone-5,5'-disulfonate sodium)

Benzophenone-12 (2-hydroxy-4-N-octoxy benzophenone)

Other UV Blockers

Amyl p-methoxy cinnamate

Octyl p-methoxy cinnamate

Para-amino Benzoic Acid

Chemical Formula

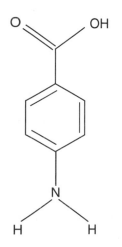

Synonyms
PABA • 4-aminobenzoic acid • p-aminobenzoic acid • ethoxylated ethyl 4-aminobenzoic acid (PEG-25 PABA)

Description
White powder.

    Para-amino benzoic acid (PABA) is considered to be in the B-complex vitamin family. The human body can make it from folic acid, since PABA forms the middle part of that vitamin:

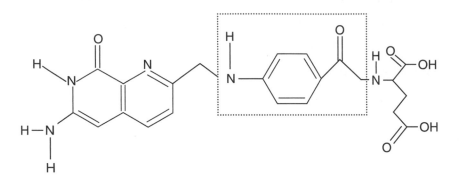

Folic acid, showing PABA inside

This means that in the strictest sense, PABA is not a vitamin, because the body can manufacture it. But in this sense, too, vitamin A is not technically a vitamin, as the body makes that from beta-carotene.

Bacteria in the intestines produce folic acid if there is PABA present. Microbes need PABA, but it is not strictly necessary for humans. A class of drugs that simulate PABA, sulfa drugs, can fool the microbes into trying to use them instead of PABA, which causes them to die. This is why people taking sulfa drugs are advised not to take PABA at the same time.

Uses

PABA is taken orally in vitamin supplements. However, its widest use is as a sunscreen. Taking it orally will not protect a person from the sun; as a sunscreen PABA acts as a topical dye that absorbs ultraviolet light. To block UV rays from the sun, a person needs to paint it directly onto the skin.

PABA is acidic, which means it can sting if it gets in the eyes. Some people are sensitive to PABA when it is applied to their skin. PABA also darkens and can stain clothing. For these reasons, modified forms of PABA have become popular as sunscreens. PABA can be reacted with long-chain alcohols to form PABA esters, such as polyethylene glycol 25 PABA:

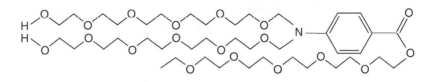

PEG-25 PABA ester

This PABA molecule eliminates the irritation and staining problems. Other PABA esters are glycerol PABA, padimate A, and padimate O.

 Chemistry Lesson

Molecules absorb light when the light's wavelength is just the right length to cause electrons in the molecule to vibrate in time with the light. The electrons resonate in the molecule.

In some molecules, the electrons are not bound to a single atomic nucleus but instead roam free across several nuclei in what are called resonance bonds. You may notice that sometimes a six-sided ring is shown with alternating double and single bonds, while at other times it is shown with a circle inside. Both forms are showing the same thing. The circle just draws attention to the fact that the bonds don't really alternate between double and single—they are more like one and a half bonds. On average, the electron spends half of the time in one place, and half in the other.

In para-amino benzoic acid, there is another resonance structure right next to the six sided ring. It is a carboxyl group, shown with a single bond between carbons, and a double bond between the carbon and the oxygen. This is also a place where the electron can bounce around between the three nuclei.

It is even possible for an electron to move back and forth across all of the resonance bonds—from one end of the molecule to another. This lets the electron slosh back and forth like water in a bathtub. In the case of para-amino benzoic acid, the rhythm of the sloshing matches the frequency of UV-B light. The electron can move in time with the light wave and absorb its energy. The energy is later released as photons of longer wavelength light such as heat. Knowing this, chemists can design other molecules that have resonance structures that will catch UV-B rays. One such molecule is benzophenone, and a derivative called benzophenone-3, also known as oxybenzone.

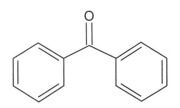

Benzophenone

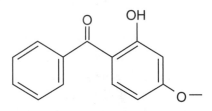

Benzophenone-3 (oxybenzone)

Notice that both molecules have the six-sided ring, called a benzine ring, and a carboxyl group (the carbon-oxygen double bond). These molecules also protect against UV-A. You can see that they have longer chains of resonance bonds, which means that they will resonate at longer wavelengths.

Getting more creative with the chemistry, a chemist can add other desirable features to these molecules. Adding long chains of hydrocarbons can help it mix better with suntan oils to spread more easily on the skin. The resonance bonds can be modified a little bit to get a broader absorption range, expanding into the longer wave UV-A region.

Such a designer molecule is octocrylene and a similar one known as avobenzone.

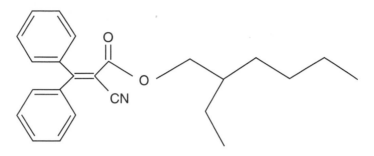

Octocrylene

Other molecules with the benzine ring and carboxyl group also have side chains added to make them better sunscreens. Two popular ones are 2-ethylhexyl salicylate:

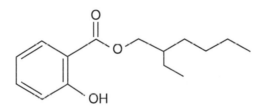

2-ethylhexyl salicylate

and homomethyl salicylate, also known as homosalate:

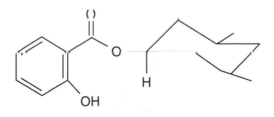

Homomethyl salicylate

Other salicylates used as sunscreens are 4-isopropylbenzyl salicylate, and triethanolamine salicylate, which goes by the trade name Trolamine Salicylate.

Another class of UV-B absorbers is the cinnamates.

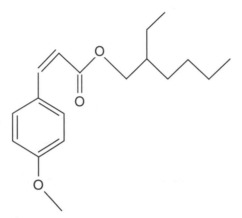

Octyl methoxycinnamate

These molecules are not water soluble, are able to stick to the skin well, and are highly effective in water-resistant sunscreens. Others in this family are isopentenyl-4-methoxycinnamate, also known as isoamyl 4-methoxycinnamate, and cinoxate.

As you can see, there are many molecules that will absorb ultraviolet light. There are many more in use than I have described here. But they all have resonance bonds in common.

Focus: Sunscreen

We love the sun. We complain about rainy days, and we look forward to summers at the beach. But we hate sunburns, wrinkled skin, and melanomas. All of those nasty things are the result of the ultraviolet rays that come with the warmth and light of sunshine.

There are a large number of chemicals used to block ultraviolet light, either to protect the user's skin or to protect a product from being damaged (colors fading, scents decomposing, etc.) Some are vitamins, such as PABA. Some are opaque powders used in creams, such as zinc oxide and titanium dioxide. Others, such as benzophenone, are designed to be invisible (they don't block visible light).

There are two ways in which chemicals can protect the skin from ultraviolet light: they can either absorb the light or reflect the light. Zinc oxide and titanium dioxide reflect or scatter light of many frequencies, from infrared through ultraviolet. That is why these chemicals appear opaque white.

If you don't want to paint yourself white, you can paint yourself with a color that absorbs ultraviolet light but is transparent to visible light.

Ultraviolet light is often divided into two types: UV-A, which has a longer wavelength (320–360 nm), and UV-B, which has a shorter wavelength (280–320 nm). Shorter wavelengths mean higher energies. UV-B is more damaging than UV-A. Some UV blockers are optimized to block the shorter wavelengths while letting the longer wavelengths get through. SPF (sun protection factor) numbers only describe UV-B protection. A high SPF can still let UV-A through. UV-C is the shortest wavelength of ultraviolet light, but it is effectively screened out by the ozone layer of the atmosphere. Because governments only allow certain percentages of each UV-absorbing compound, the higher SPF formulations generally have several UV absorbers in them.

UV-B causes sunburn, but UV-A damages collagen (connective tissue) and blood vessels, causing aging effects such as wrinkled skin.

Finally, sunscreens block the body's ability to make vitamin D from sunlight. If you are using sunscreen a lot, or if you do not get much sun, a doctor may advise you to add supplemental vitamin D to your diet.

Zinc Oxide

Chemical Formula
ZnO

Description
White powder.

Uses
Zinc oxide is a white powder that makes a very opaque paste when mixed with water or oils. It is used as a sunblock and as a colorant in toothpastes and cosmetics. Zinc oxide is used in many of the same products as titanium dioxide.

Titanium Dioxide

Chemical Formula
TiO_2

Description
White powder.

Uses
Titanium dioxide makes a very opaque paste when mixed with water or oils. It is used as a sunblock and as a colorant in toothpastes and cosmetics. Titanium dioxide is used in many of the same products as zinc oxide.

Color Stabilizers

Sulfur Dioxide

Chemical Formula
SO_2

Description
Acrid gas produced when sulfur is burned in air.

Uses
Sulfur dioxide is a reducing bleach and can counter the effects of oxidizing bleaches, thus preserving color in fruits dried in the sun. The combination of fruit acids and ultraviolet light would otherwise react with the colorful compounds, making the fruit pale.

Sulfur dioxide is produced by burning sulfur in air for preserving fruit, or by reacting sodium bisulfite in water as part of the process to make products such as wine.

Sulfur dioxide also kills yeasts, molds, and bacteria.

Sodium Bisulfite

Chemical Formula
$NaHSO_3$

Synonyms
Monosodium sulfite • sodium hydrogen sulfite • sodium sulhydrate • sulfurous acid • sodium salt

Description
Clear or milky white liquid with a sulfurous odor.

Uses
Sodium bisulfite is used in almost all commercial wines to prevent oxidation and preserve flavor. It releases sulfur dioxide gas when added to water or products containing water. The sulfur dioxide kills yeasts, fungi, and bacteria in grape juice before fermentation. When the sulfur dioxide levels have subsided, after about twenty-four hours, fresh yeast is added for fermentation.

Sodium bisulfite is often combined with an acid such as citric acid to make it produce gas faster. It is also used to sterilize winemaking equipment. It is later added to bottled wine to prevent oxidation, which would change the wine to vinegar and cause it to turn brown. The sulfur dioxide displaces oxygen in the bottle and dissolves in the wine. Without it oxidized wine can turn orange or brown and taste like raisins or cough syrup.

In fruit canning, sodium bisulfite is used to kill microbes and to prevent the browning caused by oxidation.

Antioxidants

Tocopherols

Chemical Formula

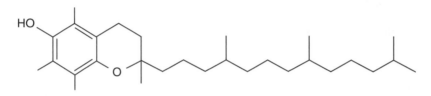

α-tocopherol

Synonyms
Vitamin E

Description
Light yellow liquid.

Uses
Vitamin E is added to some food products as a nutrient, but it is better known for its antioxidant properties, which protect oils and fats from oxidation.

Tocopherols come in various forms only slightly different from the α-tocopherol shown in the structural formula above. Its β and γ forms differ in where the methyl groups are attached to the ring structure. An ingredients list may single out the α form, or may just list "mixed tocopherols."

Ascorbic Acid

Chemical Formula

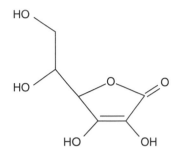

Synonyms
Vitamin C

Description
Sour-tasting white powder.

Ascorbic acid—vitamin C—is an essential nutrient that the human body cannot manufacture from other compounds. It is needed for the formation of collagen, the protein that makes up connective tissue, and is essential to muscles, bones, cartilage, and blood vessels. It is a strong antioxidant, preventing damage from oxygen free radicals.

Uses
Ascorbic acid is added to many foods for its nutritive value. It is used extensively as an antioxidant to prevent flavors and colors from being damaged by oxidation. It is often used in canned or frozen fruits to prevent the browning that accompanies oxidation. While not as powerful an antioxidant as sodium bisulfite, it has a better nutritional reputation.

An isomer (molecule with the same number and type of atoms but in a different formation) of ascorbic acid called erythorbic acid is often used as a less expensive antioxidant than ascorbic acid. It has little or no effect as a vitamin, but it has the same antioxidant properties.

To make ascorbic acid soluble in fats, it is reacted with fatty acids, such as palmitic acid, to form ascorbyl palmitate. This is used to prevent oxidation in fats and oils.

Erythorbic Acid

See Ascorbic Acid entry, page 15.

Butylated Hydroxyanisole

Chemical Formula
$CH_3OC_6H_3(OH)C(CH_3)_3$

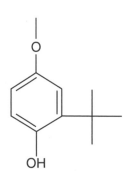

Synonyms
BHA • 2-tert-butyl-4-hydroxyanisole • 3-tert-butyl-4-hydroxyanisole

Description
White or slightly yellow waxy solid.

Uses
BHA is an antioxidant. It reacts with oxygen free radicals. It can thus slow down the rate at which ingredients in a product oxidize in direct contact with air, a process that can cause changes in the taste or color. BHA can be added to the food itself, or to the packaging material, and it is used primarily to prevent fats from becoming rancid.

Butylated Hydroxytoluene

Chemical Formula

$C_6H_2(OH)(CH_3)[C(CH_3)_3]_2$

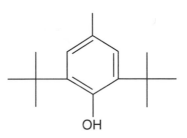

Synonyms

BHT • 2,6-di-tert-butyl-4-methylphenol • dibutylated hydroxytoluene

Description

White crystals or crystalline powder.

Uses

BHT is an antioxidant. It reacts with oxygen free radicals. It can thus slow down the rate at which ingredients in a product oxidize in direct contact with air, a process that can cause changes in the taste or color. BHT can be added to the food itself, or to the packaging material, and it is used primarily to prevent fats from becoming rancid.

Honey

Chemical Formula

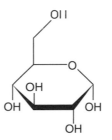

Glucose

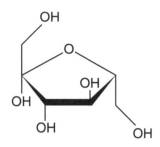

Fructose

Description
Viscous yellow liquid.

Uses
Honey is primarily fructose and glucose (in that order), with a little sucrose (about 1 percent), less than 10 percent other sugars, and about 17 percent water.

Honey's water content is high enough that it remains liquid, but low enough to make it thick and prevent spoilage. Because it contains relatively little water, microorganisms that encounter it die as the water in them is extracted by osmosis. In addition, as honey is diluted with water, a chemical reaction between glucose, water, and oxygen produces small amounts of hydrogen peroxide and gluconic acid. The slow release of hydrogen peroxide makes honey a mild antiseptic. The acidity of honey also reduces the number of organisms that can live in it.

Honey is mostly used as a sweetener, but it can also function as an antiseptic for wounds and as a preservative.

Sodium Citrate

Chemical Formula

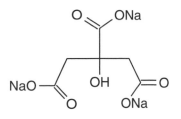

Synonyms
Trisodium citrate

Description
White odorless crystals.

Uses
Sodium citrate is used in ice cream to keep the fat globules from sticking together. Citrates and phosphates both have this property. It is also an anticoagulant.

As a buffering agent, sodium citrate helps maintain pH levels in soft drinks.

As a sequestering agent, it attaches to calcium ions in water, which keeps them from interfering with detergents and soaps.

Compounds with similar functions are sodium carbonate, sodium EDTA, phosphoric acid, pentasodium pentetate, tetrasodium etidronate, and tetrasodium pyrophosphate.

Lecithin

Chemical Formula

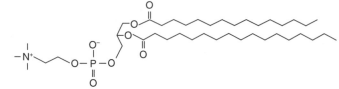

Synonyms
Phosphatidylcholine

Description
Light brown or yellow solid.

Lecithin is a phospholipid, a class of compounds that make up cell membranes throughout the body. It is produced in the liver if the diet contains enough of the raw ingredients.

Uses
Lecithin is widely used as an emulsifying agent, allowing oil and water to mix. It is used in ice creams, salad dressings, and cosmetics, and it is the main ingredient in nonstick cooking sprays. Lecithin is the emulsifier in egg yolks that allows the oil and water to mix to make mayonnaise.

Lecithin is also an antioxidant, helping to keep fats from going rancid (but in the process, going rancid itself).

Lecithin is often taken as a dietary supplement, since it contains the B vitamin choline.

Propyl Gallate

Chemical Formula

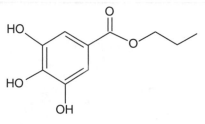

Synonyms
Gallic acid • propyl ester • N-propyl gallate • propyl 3,4,5-trihydroxy-benzoate

Description
Beige powder.

Propyl gallate is an antioxidant. It protects against oxidation by hydrogen peroxide and oxygen free radicals in a catalytic manner similar to superoxide dismutase.

Uses
Propyl gallate is used to protect oils and fats in products from oxidation. It is used in foods, cosmetics, hair products, adhesives, and lubricants.

It is synergistic with ascorbyl palmitate.

Antimicrobials

Sodium Benzoate

Chemical Formula

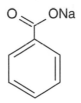

Synonyms
Benzoate of soda

Description
White powder or crystals.

Sodium benzoate converts to benzoic acid in acidic mixtures. Benzoic acid has good antimicrobial features but does not dissolve well in water, whereas sodium benzoate dissolves very well in water.

Uses

Sodium benzoate is used in acidic foods and products to control bacteria, mold, yeasts, and other microbes. It interferes with their ability to make energy.

Because it only converts to benzoic acid in acidic environments, it is not used for its antimicrobial action unless the pH is 3.6 or below. In the food industry, it is used in items such as jams, salad dressing, juices, pickles, and carbonated drinks.

It is also used as a corrosion inhibitor in automotive antifreeze products.

Benzoic Acid

Chemical Formula

Synonyms

Benzenecarboxylic acid • carboxybenzene • phenyl carboxylic acid • phenylformic acid

Description

White powder or crystals with a strong odor.

Uses

Benzoic acid has good antimicrobial features, but because it does not dissolve well in water, sodium benzoate is often used. Sodium benzoate converts to benzoic acid in acidic solutions, and dissolves very well in water.

Benzoic acid is an ingredient in toothpastes and mouthwashes, cosmetics, and deodorants.

Potassium Sorbate

Chemical Formula

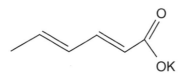

Description
White crystals.

Uses
Potassium sorbate is a polyunsaturated fatty acid salt. It is used to inhibit molds, yeasts, and fungi in many foods, including cheese, wine, and baked goods. It is the potassium salt of sorbic acid.

Sorbic Acid

Chemical Formula

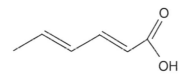

Description
White crystalline powder.
    Sorbic acid is a polyunsaturated fat.

Uses
Sorbic acid is used to inhibit molds, yeasts, and fungi in foods such as cheese, wine, and baked goods. It reacts with potassium to make potassium sorbate, and with calcium to make calcium sorbate, both of which are used as antifungals.

Natamycin

Chemical Formula

$C_{33}H_{47}NO_{13}$

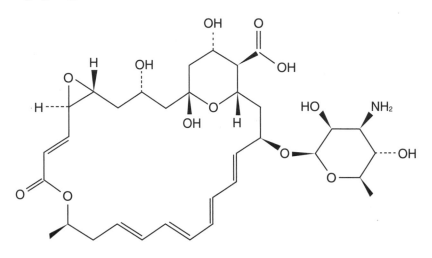

Synonyms
Pimaricin • natacyn

Description
White powder.

Uses
Natamycin is a fungicide used to keep cheese from getting moldy. It works by making holes in the cell membranes of fungi, so their insides leak out. It is produced by *Streptomyces natalensis* bacteria.

It is applied to cut slices of cheese by dipping or spraying. Some manufacturers use it in the wax coating on cheese rinds instead of on the cheese itself. In grated cheese, a dry mixture is used, usually with cellulose to prevent caking.

Triclosan

Chemical Formula

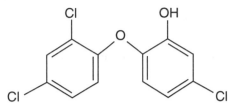

Synonyms
2,4,4′-trichloro-2′-hydroxydiphenyl ether • 5-chloro-(2,4-dichlorophe-noxy)phenol • trichloro-2′-hydroxydiphenyl ether • CH-3565 • Lexol 300 • Irgasan DP 200

Description
White powder.

Uses
Triclosan is a broad-spectrum antibacterial and antifungal agent. It is an ingredient in toothpastes and mouthwashes, detergents, laundry soaps, and cosmetics. It kills germs by interfering with the enzyme necessary for fatty-acid synthesis.

It is related to hexachlorophene in structure.

Triclocarban

Chemical Formula

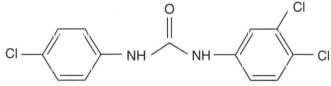

Synonyms
Trichlorocarbanilide • N-(4-chlorophenyl)-N′-(3,4-dichlorophenyl) urea

Description
White crystals or powder.

Uses
Triclocarban is used as an antibacterial and antifungal agent in disinfectants, soaps, and other household products.

Hexachlorophene

Chemical Formula

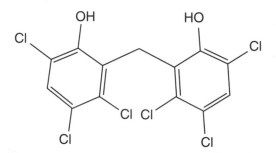

Synonyms
Hexachlorophane • hexachlorophen • hexophene • phisohex

Description
White powder.

Uses
Hexachlorophene is a broad-spectrum antibacterial agent. It is used in hospital scrubs, shampoos, and deodorants.

Once widely used in over-the-counter products, hexachlorophene is now available by prescription only, due to incidents of overdose in infants in France during the 1970s. It has been largely replaced by the related compound triclosan.

Acetic Acid

Chemical Formula

Synonyms
Vinegar

Description
Sour-tasting clear liquid.

Uses
Acetic acid, in the form of vinegar, is used to preserve foods such as pickles. It also provides the sour taste for salad dressings and mayonnaise.

Acetic acid is a fungicide and is used in cleaning products to remove calcium deposits left behind by hard water.

Sodium Chloride

Chemical Formula
NaCl

Synonyms
Salt

Description
White cubic crystals with a characteristic salty odor.

Uses
Salt is used as an essential nutrient and a flavoring in food. It is also used in products to change their properties. In breads, it moderates the growth of yeast, and strengthens gluten. In ice cream and frozen

foods, it lowers the freezing point of water. In cured meats, it acts as a preservative by attracting moisture out of the cells of microbes, which causes them to die. It also acts as a tenderizer by helping the proteins bind to water. It develops the color in preserved meats so they don't look gray. And by binding proteins to water it keeps sausage and other ground or chopped meats from falling apart. In shampoo, it is used to adjust the final viscosity of the product.

Focus: Table Salt

 Salt has been a precious commodity throughout most of human history. Rome's armies were paid in salt, which is the origin of the word *salary*. Salt is a seasoning, an essential nutrient, and a very important preservative. Table salt is sodium chloride combined with iodine sources (for nutrition), stabilizers for the iodine, and anti-caking compounds to prevent it from absorbing water from the air so it can pour freely.

Potassium Iodide

Potassium iodide is added as a nutrient to prevent goiter, a thyroid problem caused by lack of iodine, and to prevent a form of mental retardation associated with iodine deficiency. A project started by the Michigan State Medical Society in 1924 promoted the addition of iodine to table salt, and by the mid-1950s three-quarters of U.S. households used only iodized salt. Potassium iodide makes up 0.06 percent to 0.01 percent of table salt by weight. Sometimes cuprous iodide—iodide of copper—is used instead as the source of iodine.

Glucose (Dextrose)

Glucose is a sugar (the main sugar in corn syrup), and is added in small amounts (0.04 percent) to salt to prevent the potassium iodide from breaking down into iodine, which would evaporate away through sublimation. Other potassium iodide stabilizers include sodium bicarbonate (baking soda), sodium carbonate, and sodium thiosulfate.

Calcium Silicate

Calcium silicate is an anticaking additive. Salt is hygroscopic, meaning it absorbs water from the air. This water dissolves the salt, and the resulting saltwater combines with the remaining salt, cementing the grains together into a solid mass. Calcium silicate absorbs moisture from the air better than salt, but does not dissolve in the water it absorbs. This protects the salt from caking, and ensures that it pours freely. Less than 0.5 percent is generally used, so in very humid weather, the salt may still become lumpy.

Other anticaking ingredients include ferric ammonium citrate, silicon dioxide, sodium ferrocyanide, magnesium silicate, magnesium carbonate, propylene glycol, aluminum calcium silicate, sodium aluminosilicate (also called sodium silicoaluminate), and calcium phosphate.

Sugars

Chemical Formula

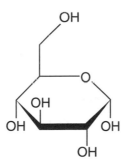

Glucose

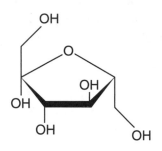

Fructose

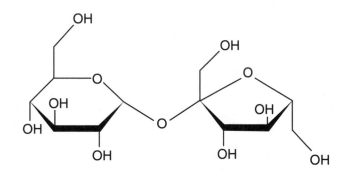

Sucrose

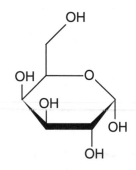

Galactose

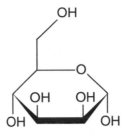

Mannose

Synonyms

Dextrose • invert sugar • corn syrup • high-fructose corn syrup

Description

White crystals or powder.

Uses

Sugars are used as sweeteners, as thickeners, and as structural elements in foods (e.g., to make granola cruchy and hard candies hard).

Table sugar is sucrose. It is made from two simpler sugars called glucose and fructose. Glucose is sometimes called dextrose. Glucose is a little less sweet than sucrose, and fructose is sweeter than sucrose. When sucrose is heated in the presence of an acid, such as vinegar or lemon juice, it breaks down into glucose and fructose, and the resulting syrup is sweeter than sucrose. The syrup is called "invert sugar."

Simple sugars can join to form long chains. Glucose units can chain up to form amylose:

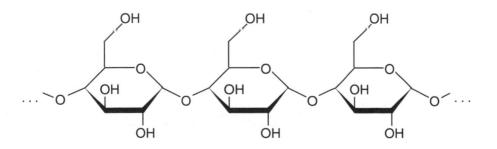

Amylose

the starch in corn, or cellulose:

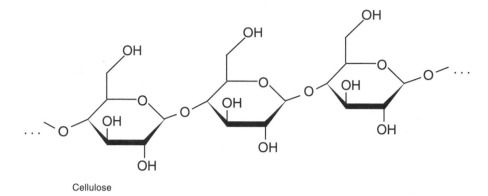

Cellulose

the molecule that forms the structure of plants.

Amylose can be broken down into its simple glucose units using enzymes. The result is called corn syrup. More processing, using enzymes that convert glucose into fructose, yields high-fructose corn syrup. The mixture of glucose and fructose is similar to that in sucrose and invert sugar, and it is sweeter than plain corn syrup.

There are many different types of simple sugars, and they can combine into many more types of complex sugars. The backbone of DNA is a chain made of sugars.

Focus: Sweeteners

What would life be like if nothing was sweet?

There are many sweeteners available today. Some are nutritive sweeteners, such as sugar; others are non-nutritive, such as saccharin; and still others fall somewhere in between, as they may have fewer calories than sugar, or be poorly metabolized in the body, or both.

Here is a list of sweeteners sorted according to how sweet they taste:

Name	% as Sweet as Sucrose (Table Sugar)
Neotame	800,000
Sucralose	60,000
Saccharin	30,000
Acesulfame potassium	20,000
Aspartame	16,000
Fructose	170
Invert sugar	120
High-fructose corn syrup	120
Xylitol	100
Tagatose	92
Maltitol	90
Glucose	75
Sorbitol	55
Mannitol	50
Maltose	45
Trehalose	45
Regular corn syrup	40
Lactose	15

The non-nutritive sweeteners stand out because they are so much sweeter than sugar.

Sugar is a disaccharide, two simple sugars in one molecule. The two simple sugars are glucose and fructose. Glucose is not as sweet as sugar, but fructose is much sweeter. This is why high-fructose corn syrup is sweeter than sugar, and why breaking the sugars in sucrose apart into glucose and fructose (making invert sugar) results in a sweeter mixture.

Adding a hydrogen or two to a sugar makes a sugar alcohol. The sugar alcohols xylitol, maltitol, sorbitol, and mannitol are all used as sweeteners in food. They are not absorbed well by the body, and they don't have as many calories as sugar. As with any food that is not absorbed well, too much can have laxative effects.

Sugar alcohols occur naturally in many foods. Our bodies create sugar alcohols as a normal part of metabolism. They are similar to sugar in their properties, so they can be used like sugar in cooking. Variations in their hygroscopicity (ability to absorb water from the air), their melting points, and their reactions with other ingredients determine which should be used in a particular recipe.

Sugar alcohols do not brown like sugar, and so they are used when caramelized brown color is not desired.

Disaccharides like maltose, lactose, and trehalose are used for their similarity to sucrose, but with differences in some properties, such as sweetness, melting point, or hygroscopicity.

Calcium Propionate

Chemical Formula

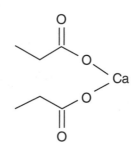

Synonyms
Calcium propanoate

Description
White crystalline solid or powder.

Uses

Calcium propionate is used in bakery products as a mold inhibitor. Propionates prevent microbes from producing the energy they need, just as benzoates do. However, unlike benzoates, propionates do not require an acidic environment.

Sodium propionate is also often used as an antifungal agent. Calcium is often preferable to sodium, both to reduce sodium levels in the diet and because calcium ions are necessary for the enzyme α-amylase to act on the starches in bread, making them available for the yeast, and improving the texture of the bread. Stale bread is caused by the starch amylose recrystallizing. The enzyme α-amylase converts some of this starch to sugars, which helps prevent recrystallization.

Sodium Propionate

Chemical Formula

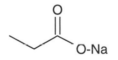

Synonyms

Sodium propanoate

Description

White crystalline solid or powder.

Uses

Sodium propionate is used in bakery products as a mold inhibitor. Like benzoates, propionates prevent microbes from producing the energy they need. However, unlike benzoates, propionates do not require an acidic environment.

Calcium propionate is often preferred as an antifungal agent, to reduce sodium levels in the diet, but also because calcium ions are necessary for the enzyme α-amylase to act on the starches in bread, making them available for the yeast, and improving the texture of the bread. Stale bread is caused by the starch amylose recrystallizing. The enzyme α-amylase converts some of this starch to sugars, which helps prevent recrystallization.

Imidazolidinyl Urea

Chemical Formula

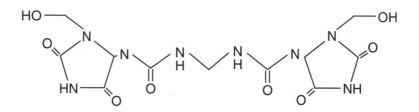

Description
White powder. Highly soluble, hygroscopic.

Uses
Imidazolidinyl urea kills gram-negative bacteria. It acts synergistically with parabens to provide a broad-spectrum antibiotic that is effective against mold, yeast, and bacteria. The combination of the two chemicals constitutes the most widely used preservative in cosmetics.

Imidazolidinyl urea works by releasing formaldehyde into the product, just like the related preservative DMDM hydantoin.

Methyl Paraben

Chemical Formula

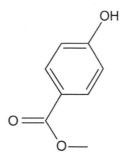

Synonyms
Methyl 4-hydroxybenzoate

Description
Colorless crystals or white powder.

Uses
Parabens are phytoestrogens found in plants such as blueberries; they are used as preservatives in food, cosmetics, sunscreens, shampoos, and many other products.

Parabens kill molds and fungi. They are used synergistically with bactericides to make broad-spectrum antimicrobials.

Related Compounds

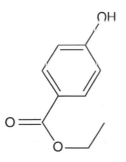

Ethyl paraben

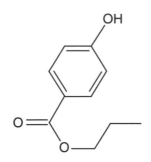

Propyl paraben

Isothiazolinone
Methylisothiazolinone
Methylchloroisothiazolinone

Chemical Formula
$C_{21}H_{38}NCl$

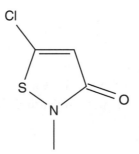

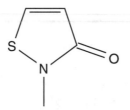

Synonyms
2-methyl-4-isothiazolin-3-one (MI) • 5-chloro-2-methyl-4-isothia-zolin-3-one (MCI) • kathon

Description
Amber liquid.

Uses
Isothiazolinones are a class of broad-spectrum biocides used as preservatives in many household and industrial products. They are used in cosmetics and shampoos as a biocide to kill fungi and bacteria. Unlike the preservatives DMDM hydantoin and imidazolidinyl urea, also commonly used in these products, isothiazolinones do not release formaldehyde, to which some people are sensitive. On the other hand, some people are sensitive to isothiazolinones.

Lactic Acid

Chemical Formula
$CH_3CH(OH)COOH$

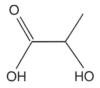

Synonyms
2-hydroxypropanoic acid • alpha-hydroxypropionic acid • 1-hydroxy-ethanecarboxylic acid • ethylidenelactic acid

Description
Colorless or slightly yellow syrupy liquid.

Uses
Lactic acid is what gives the sour taste to spoiled milk and to sauerkraut. It is used in foods to add tartness, and to preserve freshness in

foods such as Spanish olives. Though the name comes from the Latin word for *milk*, most lactic acid is produced commercially from corn fermentation.

Sodium Nitrite

Chemical Formula
$NaNO_2$

Synonyms
Nitrous acid sodium salt

Description
White or yellowish powder.

Uses
Sodium nitrite is used to fix the colors in preserved fish and meats. It is also important (along with sodium chloride) in controlling the bacterium *Clostridium botulinum*, which causes botulism. Lunch meats, hams, sausages, hot dogs, and bacon are usually preserved this way.

In medicines, it is a vasodilator, intestinal relaxant, bronchodilator, and an antidote to cyanide and hydrogen sulfide poisoning.

Sodium nitrite is produced in the human body by the action of saliva on sodium nitrate, and is important in controlling bacteria in the stomach, to prevent gastroenteritis. The body produces more sodium nitrite than is consumed in food.

Sodium nitrite can react with proteins in the stomach or during cooking, especially in high heat (such as frying bacon), to form carcinogenic N-nitrosamines. To prevent this, ascorbic acid or erythorbic acid is commonly added to cured meats.

During the curing process, some of the nitrites are converted to nitric oxide. This combines with the myoglobin proteins in the muscle of the meat to form the deep red nitric oxide myoglobin, which causes cured meats such as ham to turn pink during the smoking process.

Nitrites prevent foods from getting rancid by preventing the formation of toxic maldonadehyde, which is formed as foods get rancid.

Sodium Nitrate

Chemical Formula
$NaNO_3$

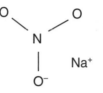

Synonyms
Soda nitre • chile saltpeter • sodium saltpeter • nitratine • nitric acid sodium salt

Description
White crystals.

Uses
Sodium nitrate has been used for centuries to cure meat. Bacterial action during curing converts the sodium nitrate into sodium nitrite, which kills the bacteria that cause botulism, and combines with the myoglobin in the meat to form the pink color associated with ham.

These days, sodium nitrite replaces most of the sodium nitrate used in cured meats, except for that used in slow-cured country ham.

DMDM Hydantoin

Chemical Formula

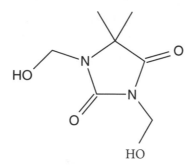

Synonyms
1,3-bis(hydroxymethyl)-5,5-dimethylimidazolidine-2,4-dione

Description
Clear liquid.

DMDM hydantoin is a preservative that works by releasing formaldehyde into the product.

Uses
DMDM hydantoin is used in shampoos and cosmetics to prevent molds, mildews, and bacterial spoilage.

Another formaldehyde-releasing preservative is imidazolidinyl urea (see page 36).

Glycols

Chemical Formulas

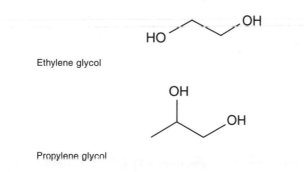

Ethylene glycol

Propylene glycol

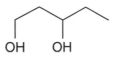

Butylene glycol

Synonyms
Ethylene glycol: ethanediol • dihydroxyethane
Propylene glycol: propanediol • dihydroxypropane
Butylene glycol: butanediol • dihydroxybutane

Description
Clear liquids.

Uses
Ethylene glycol is common in automotive antifreeze mixtures. Because of its toxicity, it is sometimes replaced by propylene glycol, which is FDA approved for use in food, and is considered "generally accepted as safe." Ethylene glycol has a sweet taste, and accidental poisoning in children is a danger.

Propylene glycol and butylene glycol are often used as humectants (moisturizers) as they are hygroscopic (they draw moisture from the air).

Propylene glycol is what is used in artificial smoke or fog machines. It is also used as a preservative.

2-bromo-2-nitropropane-1,3-diol

Chemical Formula

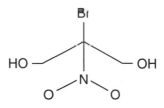

Synonyms
Bactrinol-100 • b-bromo-b-nitrotrimethyleneglycol

Description
White to pale yellow crystalline powder.

Uses
This ingredient is a bactericide used in sunscreens, hair conditioners, paints, disinfectants, and water-treatment plants.

Buffers

Some chemicals have a very nice property of maintaining the pH of a substance they are added to. If the substance becomes more acidic, the buffer ingredient shows its alkaline side and neutralizes the acid. If the substance becomes more alkaline, the acid side of the buffer neutralizes it.

Sodium Citrate

See entry, page 19.

Aminomethyl Propanol

Chemical Formula

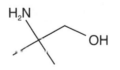

Synonyms
AMP • AMP-95 • 2-amino-2-methyl-1-propanol • isobutanolamine • amino-2-methylpropanol • hydroxymethyl-2-propylamine

Description
Colorless or slightly yellow combustible liquid.

Uses
AMP is used as an emulsifier and a buffering agent. It controls the water solubility of the resin film in hairsprays, and makes the finished film more resistant to humidity.

AMP forms a gel with long-chain acrylic polymers.

Tetrasodium Pyrophosphate

Chemical Formula
$Na_4O_7P_2$

Synonyms
Sodium pyrophosphate • TSPP • tetrasodium diphosphate

Description
Colorless transparent crystals or white powder.

Uses
Tetrasodium pyrophosphate is used as a pH buffer (a substance that maintains a particular acidity level), and as a dough conditioner in soy-based meat alternatives. It promotes binding of proteins to water, binding the soy particles together, and is used for the same purpose in chicken nuggets and imitation crab and lobster products.

It is an emulsifier, and a source of phosphorus as a nutrient.

It also is used in toothpastes, as a buffer, an emulsifier, and a detergent aid. It is the "tartar control" agent. It removes calcium and magnesium from the saliva, so they can't deposit on the teeth.

It is a thickening agent in instant puddings.

It is a water softener in detergents, and an emulsifier to suspend oils and prevent them from redepositing on clothing in the wash. As a water softener, it combines with magnesium to sequester it from the detergent and keep it from precipitating onto clothing.

As a detergent additive, it can also reactivate detergents or soaps that have combined with calcium to make an insoluble scum. The TSPP sequesters the calcium, replacing it with sodium, which reactivates the detergent or soap, and yet keeps the calcium from precipitating out of solution.

Because phosphates cause *eutrophication* of water (algae grow because of the fertilizing power of phosphates), it is seldom used as a detergent additive except in toothpastes.

Phosphoric Acid

Chemical Formula
H_3PO_4

Description
White solid.

Uses
Phosphoric acid is used in soft drinks, jams, jellies, and cheeses to add a tart (acid) flavor.

The sodium salt of phosphoric acid, sodium phosphate (NaH_2PO_4), is weakly acidic, and is used with sodium bicarbonate to make baking powders. Other acids used in baking powder are fumaric acid and tartaric acid.

Chelating or Sequestering Agents (Water Softeners)

3

The word *chelating* comes from the Latin word for claws, *chelae*, like the claws of a crab. A chelating agent grabs on to another molecule, like a crab's claw, and prevents it from reacting with other molecules.

Chelating (sometimes called sequestering) agents include water-softening agents that lock up the calcium and magnesium in hard water so that they don't interfere with soaps and detergents. Other chelating agents are added to foods to lock up metals, such as nickel and copper, to prevent them from reacting, or as a medicine to remove mercury or other toxic heavy metals from the body.

Ethylene Diamine Tetra Acetic Acid

Chemical Formula

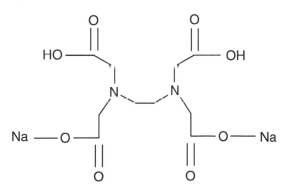

Sodium EDTA

Synonyms
Sodium EDTA • calcium EDTA

Description
White crystalline powder.

Uses
Sodium or calcium EDTA binds to metals, such as nickel, copper, and iron, making them unavailable to react with other ingredients in a product, or with compounds in the human body.

EDTA sequesters calcium and magnesium from hard water, preventing them from forming insoluble soap films (scum) with soaps and detergents. Chelators are sometimes used to sequester metal ions that interfere with dyes and perfumes.

EDTA also is used to treat lead and mercury poisoning, as it can lock up those metals so they can do no harm in the body.

Compounds with similar functions are sodium carbonate, pentasodium pentetate, sodium citrate, phosphoric acid, tetrasodium etidronate, and tetrasodium pyrophosphate.

Diethylene Triamine Pentaacetic Acid

Chemical Formula

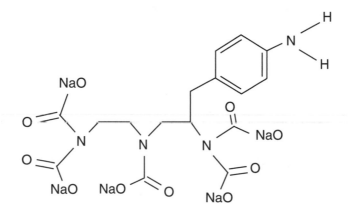

Synonyms

Pentasodium pentetate • (((carboxymethyl)imino)bis(ethylenenitrilo))tetraacetic acid • pentasodium salt

Description

White crystals.

Diethylene triamine pentaacetic acid is a chelating agent that sequesters metal ions so they cannot combine with other ingredients in a product.

Uses

Diethylene triamine pentaacetic acid is used in soaps as a water softener, and to protect dyes and perfumes from combining with metals in solution.

Compounds with similar functions are sodium carbonate, sodium EDTA, sodium citrate, phosphoric acid, tetrasodium etidronate, and tetrasodium pyrophosphate.

Phosphoric Acid

See entry, page 47.

Sodium Citrate

See entry, page 19.

Tetrasodium Pyrophosphate

See entry, page 46.

Tetrasodium Etidronate

Chemical Formula

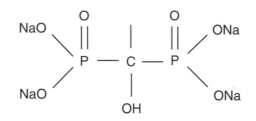

Synonyms
Tetrasodium (1-hydroxyethylidene) bisphosphonate

Description
Clear or pale yellow liquid.

Tetrasodium etidronate, and the related disodium etidronate,

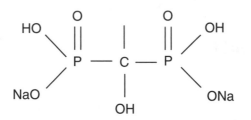

are chelating agents and sequestering agents that attach to metal ions to keep them from reacting with other compounds in a mixture, and to prevent them from precipitating out of solution as insoluble scums.

Uses
Tetrasodium etidronate is used as a water softener in soaps to prevent soap scum and bathtub rings by locking up the calcium and magnesium in the water.

Compounds with similar functions are sodium carbonate, sodium EDTA, sodium citrate, phosphoric acid, and tetrasodium pyrophosphate.

Sodium Carbonate

Chemical Formula
Na_2CO_3

Synonyms
Soda • soda ash • washing soda

Description
White hygroscopic powder or crystals.

Uses
Sodium carbonate is used in detergent formulas as a water softener, to lock up calcium and magnesium from the water. Calcium and magnesium would otherwise combine with the soap or detergents and form an insoluble scum that would stick to the clothes and the washing machine.

Compounds with similar functions are pentasodium pentetate, sodium EDTA, sodium citrate, phosphoric acid, tetrasodium etidronate, and tetrasodium pyrophosphate.

Alcohols and Phenols

This group of ingredients has many useful properties. Alcohols and phenols are very common in household products. Alcohols are good solvents and are used in perfumes and flavorings to dissolve fats and oils. Heavier alcohols with long chains of hydrocarbons act as emulsifiers and surfactants, bringing oil and water together.

Ethanol

Chemical Formula

Synonyms
Alcohol • ethyl alcohol • SD alcohol 40-B

Description
Colorless flammable liquid.

Uses
When the word *alcohol* is used alone, it refers to ethanol, the alcohol found in wine, beer, and distilled spirits. Ethanol is used as a fast-drying solvent in many products, especially cosmetics and hairsprays.

When used in products not licensed for drinking, ethanol usually occurs in the form of *denatured* alcohol, or "specially denatured" alcohol—alcohol that has been rendered unfit for drinking. You will often see "SD alcohol" mentioned on a label, sometimes followed by a number and letter, such as "40-B." This is the designation given by the U.S. Bureau of Alcohol, Tobacco, and Firearms to the denaturing method used. For example, SD-40 is ethanol denatured by adding tiny amounts of the most bitter-tasting substance known: denatonium benzoate.

Other Alcohols

There are a large number of alcohols besides ethanol. All of them have the hydroxyl group OH attached to a carbon atom. The simplest is methanol:

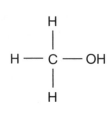

Methanol has one carbon, ethanol has two, and there are two forms of the alcohol that contain three carbons: propanol

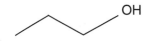

and isopropanol

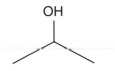

Stearyl Alcohol

Chemical Formula

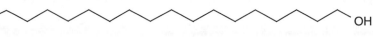

Synonyms
1-octadecanol • octadecyl alcohol

Description
White solid or flakes.

Uses
Stearyl alcohol is a nonionic surfactant used as a hair coating in shampoos and conditioners.

Stearyl alcohol also is used as an emollient (skin softener), emulsifier, and thickener in creams and lotions.

Cetyl Alcohol

Chemical Formula

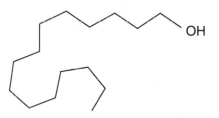

Synonyms
1-hexadecanol • hexadecyl alcohol

Description
White solid or flakes.

Uses
Cetyl alcohol is a nonionic surfactant used as a hair coating in shampoos and conditioners.

It is used as a water-based lubricant for fasteners, such as nuts and bolts.

It is used as an emollient (skin softener), emulsifier, and thickener in creams and lotions.

Glycerin

Chemical Formula

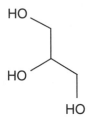

Synonyms

Glycerol • glycerine • 1,2,3 trihydroxy propane • 1,2,3 propanetriol

Description

Glycerin is a clear, sweet-tasting, somewhat viscous oily liquid.

It is manufactured from petroleum, or from glycerides in fats, often as a by-product in the production of soap.

Uses

Glycerin is hydrophilic (water-loving), and is used to keep products such as dried fruits from getting too dry, and to keep the liquid in soft fillings from escaping into crisp crusts, making them soggy. This emollient (moisturizing) effect also finds use in hand creams. It lowers the freezing point of water, and is used as an antifreeze.

Glycerin is about three-quarters as sweet as sugar, so it can reduce the need for sugar in products that require it for other reasons. In toothpaste it sweetens while keeping the paste from drying out when the cap is left off.

Glycerin is used in many skin creams and medicines, such as eye and ear drops, poison ivy creams, suppositories, and contraceptive jellies. It is also used as an emollient (skin softener) in soaps.

When glycerin reacts with nitric acid in the presence of sulfuric acid (as a drying agent) a familiar compound results:

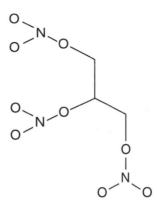

Glyceryl trinitrate

Glyceryl trinitrate is used in medicines for its effects on blood flow. Physicians use it as a coronary vasodilator for their heart patients.

As an explosive, glycerin is the principle ingredient in dynamite, under the name nitroglycerin.

Menthol

Chemical Formula

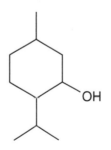

Synonyms
2-isopropyl-5-methyl-cyclohexanol

Description

Colorless crystals with a strong characteristic odor. It is the chief constituent of peppermint oil.

Uses

Menthol is a mild anesthetic and anti-irritant. It causes a cool sensation on the skin, by activating the peripheral cold receptors. It is used in cigarettes, and in topical creams for the relief of sore muscles. It also is used in cough drops, aftershave lotions, inhalers, and cooling gels.

Menthol is used as a flavoring in toothpastes, chewing gums, candies, and liquors. And it is used as a perfume in towels, handkerchiefs, deodorizers, and shampoos.

Waxes

5

Although some waxes are made from more complicated building blocks, most of what are commonly called waxes are esters. In addition to the uses discussed below, waxes were used for many years to make candles; today, however, most candles are made from long-chain hydrocarbons called paraffin, which are not true waxes.

Esters

Chemical Formula

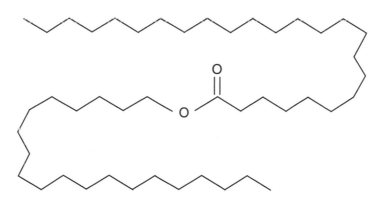

Synonyms

Beeswax (triacontanyl palmitate) • octadecyl octadecanoate (stearyl stearate) • dodecyl hexadecanoate (lauryl palmitate) • cetyl palmitate • lanolin • carnauba wax • glycol distearate • jojoba oil

Description

Waxy solids, combinations of long-chain alcohols and long-chain fatty acids.

The wax that bees make is a complicated mixture of many compounds, but about 70 percent of it is the wax made from palmitic acid, a fatty acid, and the long-chain alcohol triacontanol (melissyl alcohol).

Uses

Waxes are used in water-resistant coating on cars and furniture. They are also used in lipsticks and eyebrow pencils and in liquid soaps and shampoos to give a pearlescent effect (the tiny flakes of the wax glycol distearate reflect the light).

Lanolin is a wax made in the sebaceous glands of sheep and washed out of wool with detergents. It is used in many hair- and skin-care products.

Waxes are the principal component in traditional varnishes such as shellac, a wax made by the cochineal insect *Tachardia lacca*.

Flavorings

Flavorings can be derived from simple acids that add a sour taste to foods, or they can comprise more complex molecules, such as denatonium benzoate, which is added to products to make them so bitter that no one will accidentally ingest harmful amounts.

Acids

Acetic Acid

See entry, page 27.

Citric Acid

Chemical Formula

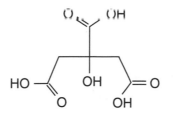

Synonyms
2-hydroxy-1,2,3-propanetricarboxylic acid

Description
Colorless, odorless, translucent crystals or powder. Strongly sour (acidic) taste.

Uses
Citric acid is used as a food additive to make foods tart, to adjust the acidity, or to mix with bicarbonates to generate carbon dioxide gas.

It is also used known for its antioxidant properties, and can be used to prevent oils from becoming rancid.

Citric acid is also highly astringent; it can be used as a skin toner.

Like the related compound sodium citrate, citric acid is often an ingredient in ice creams, where it helps keep the fat globules separate.

Lactic Acid

See entry, page 39.

Stearic Acid

Chemical Formula
$CH_3(CH_2)_{16}COOH$

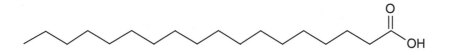

Synonyms
1-heptadecanecarboxylic acid • n-octadecanoate • n-octadecylic acid • cetylacetic acid • stearophanic acid

Description
White or yellowish solid.

Uses

Stearic acid is the most common of the long-chain fatty acids. It is found in many foods, such as beef fat and cocoa butter. It is widely used as a lubricant in soaps, cosmetics, food packaging, deodorant sticks, and toothpastes. It is also a commonly used softener in rubber.

 ## Chemistry Lesson

Stearic acid is a member of the group called fatty acids. These are hydrocarbon chains (chains made of repeated units of a carbon atom and two hydrogen atoms) with a carboxyl group at one end. A carboxyl group is the COOH in the chemical formula. It is what turns the hydrocarbon chain into an organic acid.

The carboxyl group in organic acids is reactive, and will easily lose its hydrogen to a compound that has a hydroxyl group, which is an oxygen atom joined to a hydrogen atom (OH). The H from the carboxyl group joins the OH of the hydroxyl group, and the two become HOH, more commonly known as H_2O: water. The water leaves as a separate molecule, and the two original molecules become joined at the point where the carboxyl and hydroxyl groups were.

One compound, glycerol, happens to have three hydroxyl groups. Glycerol can combine with fatty acids to form compounds called glycerides.

If there is one fatty acid, you get a monoglyceride. If there are two fatty acids, you get a diglyceride. When there are three fatty acids, you get a triglyceride.

Glycerol stearate is a monoglyceride. It is glycerol attached to stearic acid. Because it still has two free hydroxyl groups attached to the glycerol, that portion of the molecule is hydrophilic, or attracted to water. The long hydrocarbon chain of the stearic acid is hydrophobic, or attracted to oils and fats instead of water. This makes it a good emulsifying agent and surfactant. An emulsifier helps to mix oil and water in products such as mayonnaise and butter.

Diglycerides are also emulsifying agents. You will see mono- and diglycerides as ingredients in many foods that combine oil and water.

Triglycerides are fats. The fats in butter and bacon, like the fats in your body, are made of triglycerides.

Stearic acid is a saturated fatty acid. This means it has only single bonds between its carbon atoms. This means it can coil up and form into random shapes. Double bonds between carbon atoms restrict the bending of the molecule at the point of the bond, like a hinge that lets a door swing back and forth but not up and down. Triple bonds are even more restrictive, locking the joint in place three-dimensionally, like the legs of a tripod.

Unlike most saturated fats, stearic acid does not seem to increase cholesterol levels in the blood. This is because liver enzymes convert it to an unsaturated fat during digestion.

Phosphoric Acid

See entry, page 47.

Fumaric Acid

Chemical Formula

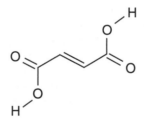

Synonyms
Allomaleic acid • 2-butenedioic acid • trans-butenedioic acid • boletic acid • lichenic acid • trans-1,2-ethenedicarboxylic acid

Description
Colorless crystals or white powder.

Uses
Fumaric acid is used as a flavoring, because it is the sourest tasting of the organic acids. Three parts of fumaric acid are as sour as five parts of citric acid.

It is also used as an antioxidant, as a mordant (a substance that helps dyes stick to fabric), and as a buffering agent (which helps maintain a particular acidity or alkalinity).

Fumaric acid is used to lower the pH (make something more acidic, which makes it taste more sour). This helps certain antimicrobial agents such as sodium benzoate and calcium propionate work more effectively. Fumaric acid also kills bacteria.

Fumaric acid breaks the sulfur-to-sulfur bonds in the elastic protein gluten in bread doughs. This makes the doughs more machineable. It also is a key ingredient in rye and sourdough breads—it makes them sourer.

Fumaric acid is used in combination with sodium bicarbonate to create delayed-action leavening agents (something that produces carbon dioxide gas to make breads rise). Since it only dissolves in warm water, the leavening action is delayed until the bread starts to bake.

Because fumaric acid is not very soluble in water, it can replace hygroscopic acids in dry mixes, and thus help keep them from caking in humid conditions.

Tartaric Acid

Chemical Formula

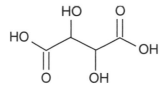

Synonyms
2,3-dihydroxybutanedioic acid

Description
White powder.

Tartaric acid is the molecule that makes unripe grapes taste sour. It is a principal flavor element in wine.

Uses

Tartaric acid is used as a flavoring agent to make foods taste sour.

The potassium salt of tartaric acid, potassium bitartrate or potassium hydrogen tartrate, is weakly acidic, and is known as cream of tartar. Since it is a dry acid, cream of tartar is used in baking powders (along with sodium bicarbonate) to produce carbon dioxide gas when added to water. Other acids used in baking powder are fumaric acid and phosphoric acid.

Esters

Methyl Vanillin

Chemical Formula

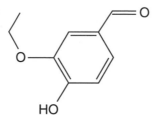

Synonyms
Vanillin • 3-methoxy-4-hydroxybenzaldehyde

Description
White to light yellow crystalline powder.

Uses
Methyl vanillin is used in flavorings, fragrances, pharmaceuticals, and perfumes. It is closely related to ethyl vanillin, a slightly larger molecule.

Because it does not have quite the same taste as the much more complex mixture of compounds found in natural vanilla extract, it is most often used with stronger flavors and scents such as chocolate, cloves, nutmeg, or cinnamon.

Ethyl Vanillin

Chemical Formula

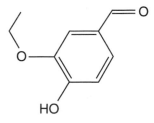

Synonyms
3-ethoxy-4-hydroxybenzaldehyde

Description
White to pale yellow powder or crystals with a characteristic odor of vanilla.

Uses
Ethyl vanillin is a synthetic compound that is three and a half times stronger in flavor than real vanilla, although the flavor is not quite the same. Because it is less expensive and keeps better during storage and transport, ethyl vanillin is used as a substitute for vanilla in foods and perfumes.

It is closely related to the slightly smaller molecule methyl vanillin.

Denatonium Benzoate

Chemical Formula

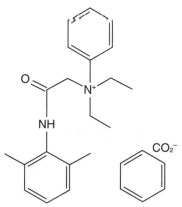

Synonyms
Bitrex

Description
White crystalline powder with an extremely bitter taste.

Uses
Denatonium benzoate is the bitterest-tasting substance known. It gets its name from *denatured* alcohol—alcohol that has been rendered unfit for drinking—and is often used in the denaturing process. Specially denatured alcohol 40, or SD-40, is ethanol that has been denatured by a tiny amount of denatonium benzoate. Denatonium benzoate is an ester of PABA, and is related to lidocaine, benzocaine, novocaine, and cocaine.

It is used in deer repellant, nail polish (to discourage nail-biting), paint, antifreeze, and windshield washing fluid (to prevent accidental ingestion), and to coat electrical cables (to prevent rats or other vermin from eating the insulation). Very dilute solutions are sometimes used to coat children's thumbs to prevent thumb sucking.

Other Flavorings

Vanilla

Chemical Formula
Vanilla is a complex mix of many compounds, such as vanillin and related esters.

Synonyms
Vanilla beans • vanilla sugar • vanilla extract

Description
Long black bean.

Vanilla is sold in many forms, such as the vanilla bean, vanilla extract, and vanilla sugar.

The vanilla bean is the fruit of the orchid *Vanilla planifolia*, a native of Mexico, but now grown in many tropical countries such as Madagascar, Tahiti, and Java. The flowers of the vanilla orchid are pollinated by local Mexican bees and hummingbirds, and until a hand pollination method was developed, the seed capsules could only be farmed in Mexico. Orchid flowers bloom once per day, and a good hand pollinator can pollinate one thousand to two thousand plants a day. The seeds ripen about nine months after they are pollinated.

The seed pods are picked when they turn yellow, and dried in the sun during the day, then placed in straw or blankets in airtight boxes to "sweat" and ferment overnight. The sun drying, boxing, and fermenting process is repeated many times for over a month, and the result is black seed pods that are then thoroughly dried, boxed, and cured for a few months before being shipped.

The long fermenting process converts several glucosides into glucose, vanillin, and other complex aromatic flavors. The vanilla beans can be further processed by extracting soluble compounds in ethanol and water mixtures, resulting in vanilla extract.

Uses

Vanilla is used in many products, usually sweetened foods, and scented products, such as perfumes and candles.

Vanilla grown in one location tastes different than that grown in another location, much like coffee, wine, and chocolate. Many confectioners claim the vanilla grown in Madagascar, known as Bourbon Vanilla, tastes the best, because of its fruity "top note." The vanilla grown in Indonesia has a simpler flavor and is used in baking, where any top notes would be removed from the product by the high heat. Mexican vanillas are often described as "spicy." Tahitian vanilla is said to have flowery, soft flavors, resembling root beer, which is a somewhat circular reference, since most root beer contains vanilla. There are also blended vanillas, mixing beans from various locations.

Monosodium Glutamate

Chemical Formula

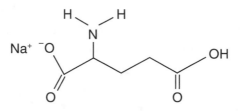

Synonyms
Sodium glutamate • MSG • l-glutamic acid • monosodium salt • hydrolyzed vegetable protein • utolyzed yeast • whey protein

Description
White crystalline powder.

MSG is the sodium salt of the amino acid glutamic acid. It is made commercially by the fermentation of molasses, but exists in many products made from fermented proteins, such as soy sauce and hydrolyzed vegetable protein.

The human tongue is sensitive to five flavors: salty, sweet, bitter, sour, and *umami*, the taste of MSG.

Glutamic acid is a component of many proteins, such as those in dairy products, meat, legumes, and mushrooms. However, only the free form of glutamic acid or glutamates has an effect on the glutamate receptors. When bound to other amino acids in a protein, it does not stimulate glutamate receptors.

Free glutamates exist in certain cheeses (such as parmesan), in tomato products, and in soy sauce. These products are often used to enhance the flavor of meat dishes. Proteins can be hydrolyzed by heat, releasing free glutamates. Cooked meats, especially grilled meats, get some of their taste from free glutamates.

Uses
MSG is used to give a meaty, savory, or brothy taste to foods by stimulating the glutamate receptors on the tongue. There are glutamate receptors in other parts of the body, notably the brain, where glutamate is a neurotransmitter.

Glutamates can be produced by fermentation of starches or sugars, but also by breaking the bonds between amino acids in proteins, leaving free amino acids. This process is done by heat or by enzymes; it is called *hydrolyzing*, because the bonds are broken by adding water.

When proteins are broken down into their constituent amino acids, the result can contain as much as 20 percent glutamates. This is why hydrolyzed vegetable protein is often listed as an ingredient in foods, to give them a meaty or savory flavor.

There is evidence that some people are sensitive to free gluta-mates. These people get headaches or other symptoms if they ingest too much. This may be related to pyridoxine (vitamin B6) deficien-cies, as this vitamin is necessary for glutamate metabolism. People with uncontrolled severe asthma may find that glutamates complicate or worsen their symptoms.

Bound glutamates in proteins are very common in food. Human breast milk contains ten times as much as cow's milk, and tomato juice contains four times as much as breast milk. However, free glutamate, as found in soy sauce or prepared foods, enters the bloodstream much faster than the glutamates bound in proteins, which are released slowly during digestion.

Sweeteners

7

Sweeteners can be anything from simple sugars to fragments of proteins, such as aspartame, that trigger the sweet receptors on our tongues, sometimes up to two hundred times as strongly as sugar itself.

Most sweeteners are forms of sugar, since sugar is very cheap and easily available. But for health reasons, more and more people are getting their sweeteners in non-nutritive form, or in the form of short proteins that are so sweet that the number of calories needed to sweeten the food is negligible.

Sucrose

See Sugars entry, page 29.

Invert Sugar

See Sugars entry, page 29.

Fructose

See Sugars entry, page 29.

High-Fructose Corn Syrup

See Sugars entry, page 29.

Neotame

Chemical Formula

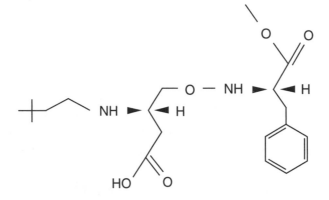

Synonyms

N-[N-(3,3-dimethylbutyl)-L-α-aspartyl]-L-phenylalanine 1-methyl ester

Description

White powder.

Neotame is an artificial sweetener designed to overcome some of the problems with aspartame. The dimethylbutyl part of the molecule was added to block the action of peptidases, enzymes that break the peptide bond between the two amino acids aspartic acid and phenylalanine. This reduces the availability of phenylalanine, eliminating the need for a warning on labels directed at people who cannot properly metabolize phenylalanine.

Neotame does not break down with the heat of cooking, another drawback to aspartame. It is also thirty times sweeter than aspartame, so less is needed to sweeten a product.

Uses

Neotame is about eight thousand times sweeter than sugar, so only 6 milligrams is needed to sweeten a typical 12-ounce soft drink.

Neotame is used in tabletop sweeteners, frozen desserts, chewing gum, candy, baked goods, fruit spreads, and ready-to-eat cereals.

Acesulfame Potassium

Chemical Formula

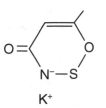

Synonyms
Acesulfame K

Description
Crystalline powder.

Acesulfame potassium is a noncaloric sweetener that is two hundred times sweeter than sugar. It is used in tabletop sweeteners, toothpastes, soft drinks, desserts, baked goods, and canned foods.

Uses
Acesulfame potassium is used with other sweeteners such as aspartame because it has a long shelf life, and tastes sweet right away. It also has a synergistic effect with other sweeteners, so less of each is necessary to achieve the same sweetness.

Aspartame

Chemical Formula

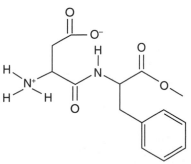

Synonyms
L-alpha-aspartyl-L-phenylalanine methyl ester

Description
White powder.

Aspartame is made from two amino acids and methanol. When it is digested, it breaks down into these three parts. Amino acids are the normal breakdown products of proteins.

Uses
Aspartame is a low-calorie sweetener used in many foods and drinks. Because it is between 160 and 200 times sweeter than sugar, only very small amounts are needed to sweeten a product. A typical 12-ounce low-calorie soft drink will have 180 milligrams of aspartame in it.

In acidic solutions at high temperatures, aspartame degrades and loses its sweetness.

Sucralose

Chemical Formula

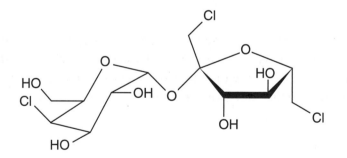

Synonyms
Splenda

Description
White crystalline powder.

Focus: Soft Drinks

Soft drinks are among the most recognized products of Western culture. Beginning as tonics for fatigue (and anything else that might be the matter with a patient), they have evolved into sweet bubbly accompaniments to hamburgers, fries, and other fast foods.

Most soft drinks are characterized by carbonated water, sugar, and caffeine. Variations in soft drinks generally advertise either flavor differences, or the absence of one or more of the three main ingredients.

Colas

The largest segment of the soft drink industry is cola. Colas were originally blends of extracts of the coca leaf and the cola nut, mixed with sugar water. The coca leaf is no longer used, but the cola nut remains in the recipes that are public and reportedly is also still in the secret Coca-Cola recipe. The cola nut comes from the Ivory Coast in West Africa, primarily from two species of trees, *Cola acuminata* and *Cola nitida*. The main active ingredients in the cola nut are the alkaloids caffeine and theobromine ("food of the gods").

Colas stimulate digestive juices, and carbonated water speeds the digestion, and this combination of effects, along with the stimulant action of the two alkaloids, can make a big difference to someone who is not feeling well.

Sweeteners

Sugar in soft drinks has been largely replaced by high-fructose corn syrup, largely because, unlike sugar, high-fructose corn syrup is not price-controlled by the U.S. government, and because it is a bit sweeter than sugar, so less is needed.

The artificial sweetener aspartame is the low-calorie sweetener of choice at the time of this writing, having replaced cyclamates and saccharin as the industry favorites. The sweeteners neotame, acesulfame, and sucralose are sometimes used as well.

Flavors

Acids are added to soft drinks for extra bite. The primary acid used in colas is phosphoric acid, while the one used in citrus-flavored drinks is usually citric acid. Carbonated water (water that has the gas carbon dioxide dissolved in it under pressure) is also mildly acidic (it is chemically carbonic acid, H_2CO_3).

Caffeine is added as a stimulant, but it has a bitter taste that is a component in many soft drinks.

Orange soda often contains glyceryl abietate, also known as glycerol esters of wood rosin and brominated vegetable oil. These help keep fatty flavors suspended in the liquid (density balancers and emulsifiers). Gums and modified food starches are also used for this purpose. Glyceryl abietate is also used in cosmetics as the waxy substance in eyebrow pencils.

Preservatives

Sodium benzoate is used as a broad-spectrum antimicrobial, inhibiting bacteria, molds, and yeasts. The high acid content of the soft drink is necessary for the preservative action. Sodium citrate buffers the acids, so the pH stays low (acidic). It also emulsifies any fats or fat-soluble compounds in the flavorings, keeping them in solution.

Potassium sorbate is added to inhibit yeasts and fungi.

Ascorbic acid (vitamin C) is used as an antioxidant.

Colors

In colas, the brown color comes from caramel coloring (burnt sugar).

Red 40 and other colors are used in fruit-flavored drinks such as orange soda.

Sucralose is the sugar sucrose with three of the hydroxyl groups replaced by chlorine atoms. In the process, the stereochemistry of the glucose half of the molecule is changed, making it more like galactose.

Sucralose is six hundred times sweeter than sugar but has no calories.

Uses
Sucralose is used in a wide variety of no-calorie and low-calorie foods, such as tabletop sweeteners, baked goods, desserts, toothpastes, mouthwashes, and diet drinks.

Saccharin

Chemical Formula

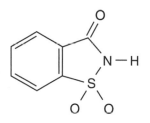

Synonyms
Sweet'N Low

Description
White, sweet-tasting powder.

Uses
Saccharin is a non-nutritive sweetener used in toothpastes, cold remedies, ice creams, and coffee-sweetening packets. Its use in soft drinks has been almost entirely replaced by aspartame.

It is about three hundred times sweeter than sugar, and passes unaltered through the body, so it has no calories.

Lactose

Chemical Formula

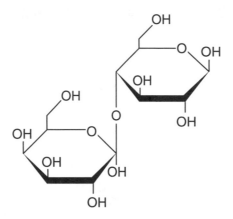

Synonyms
Milk sugar

Description
White, odorless, slightly sweet-tasting powder.

Lactose is a disaccharide, two simple sugars in one molecule. In this case, the sugars are galactose and glucose.

Uses
Lactose is mainly used as a fermentation substrate for lactic acid bacteria in dairy products, such as yogurt and cheese. These bacteria break down lactose into lactic acid, which solidifies the milk, and creates an acid environment that favors the benign lactic acid bacteria over those that are more harmful.

Poorly Absorbed Carbohydrates and Sugar Alcohols

Sorbitol

Chemical Formula

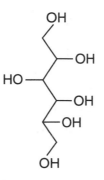

Synonyms
D-glucitol • gulitol • Neosorb

Description
White, odorless, sweet-tasting powder.

Sorbitol is a sugar alcohol. It has two thirds the calories of sugar, and is only 60 percent as sweet. It is poorly absorbed by the body, so it does not raise insulin levels as much as sugar. It does not promote tooth decay.

Sorbitol and mannitol are isomers, substances with the same chemical formula but a different shape. Sorbitol can be described as a glucose molecule with two hydrogens added. The two extra hydrogens are on either side of what used to be the double bond connecting the oxygen to the carbon, which is now a single bond. This changes the molecule just enough to make it harder for the body to absorb, while still allowing it to taste sweet on the tongue.

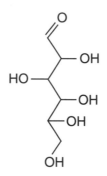

Glucose

Sorbitol occurs naturally in fruits and vegetables. Most sorbitol in foods and other products is made from corn syrup.

Uses
Sorbitol is used in low-calorie candies and in many other foods as both a sweetener and a humectant (moisture-retaining ingredient). It also is used as an emollient (skin softener) in soaps.

Mannitol

Chemical Formula

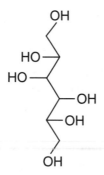

Synonyms
Manna sugar • mannite • D-mannitol • 1,2,3,4,5,6-hexanehexol

Description
White, odorless, sweet-tasting powder.

Mannitol is a sugar alcohol. It has half the calories of sugar and is half as sweet. It is poorly absorbed by the body, so it does not raise insulin levels as much as sugar does. It does not promote tooth decay.

Mannitol and sorbitol are isomers, substances with the same chemical formula but a different shape.

Uses

Mannitol is used as the dusty coating on chewing gum; it keeps the gum from absorbing moisture and getting sticky. This is due to its humectant (moisture-trapping) properties and very low hygroscopicity (meaning that it does not attract moisture from the air).

Xylitol

Chemical Formula

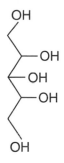

Synonyms
Wood sugar • birch sugar

Description
White, odorless, sweet-tasting powder.

Xylitol is a sugar alcohol. It has 40 percent fewer calories than sugar but is just as sweet. It is poorly absorbed by the body, so it does not raise insulin levels as much as sugar does. It does not promote tooth decay.

Uses

Xylitol is used as a sweetener in many foods, including low-calorie candies, gums, and breath mints. It prevents bacteria from adhering to cells in the mouth and gums. It also binds to calcium and aids in remineralizing tooth enamel and bones.

Nasal sprays and ear drops use xylitol to reduce the adhesion of bacteria.

Maltitol

Chemical Formula

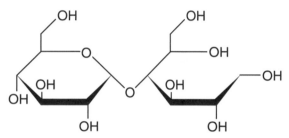

Synonyms
4-O-α-D-glucopyranosyl-D-glucitol

Description
White, odorless, sweet-tasting powder.

Maltitol is a sugar alcohol like sorbitol, mannitol, and xylitol, but it is a larger molecule. Unlike those other sugar alcohols, and menthol, maltitol does not stimulate the cold sensors in the skin, so it does not feel cool in the mouth.

Uses
Maltitol is used in reduced-calorie foods as a sweetener. It does not promote tooth decay, and so it is used to sweeten toothpastes and mouthwash. It is especially useful in low-calorie chocolate, because it is more like sugar than other sugar alcohols. It doesn't absorb water from the air, it is stable under heating, and it has a high melting point.

Hydrogenated Starch Hydrosylate

Chemical Formula
Hydrogenated starch hydrosylate is a mixture of several polyols, or sugar alcohols, such as sorbitol, maltitol, and mannitol, among others.

Synonyms
HSH

Description
Clear viscous liquid.

Hydrogenated starch hydrosylate is made from cornstarch, potato starch, or wheat starch, which is broken down into small units such as glucose, dextrin, maltodextrin, and polydextrin, by amylase enzymes in a process called hydrolyzing. Hydrolyzing breaks the bond between two glucose molecules by adding an OH to one glucose and a hydrogen to the other. The H and OH come from splitting water, hence the term *hydrolyze*, which means "to break apart using water." After the starch is broken into little pieces of glucose and short glucose chains, the pieces are converted from sugars to sugar alcohols by adding two hydrogens, using heat and pressure. The addition of hydrogen to a molecule is called hydrogenation.

If the starch is completely hydrolyzed, so that there are only single glucose molecules, then after hydrogenation the result is sorbitol. If the starch is not completely hydolyzed, then a mixture of sorbitol, maltitol, and longer-chain hydrogenated saccharides (such as maltitriitol) is produced. When there is no single dominant polyol in the mix, the compound goes by the generic name hydrogenated starch hydrosylate. If more than half of the polyols in the mixture are of one type, then the mixture is called "sorbitol syrup" or "maltitol syrup," and so forth.

Uses
Hydrogenated starch hydrosylate is used in low-calorie candies and in many other foods as both a sweetener and a humectant (moisture-retaining ingredient).

As a crystallization modifier, it can prevent syrups from forming crystals of sugar. It is used to add body and viscosity to mixtures, and can protect against damage from freezing and drying.

Hydrogenated starch hydrosylate is also used as a carrier for enzymes, colors, or flavors.

Salt Substitutes

High levels of sodium in the diet are linked to high blood pressure. Doctors often recommend that individuals who need to lower their blood pressure limit their sodium intake, but the sodium in table salt is a big part of most people's diets. They can turn to salt substitutes instead.

Doctors may also recommend increasing potassium in the diet to help lower blood pressure. Salt substitutes that contain potassium thus address the problem in two different ways.

Potassium Chloride

Chemical Formula
KCl

Synonyms
Salt

Description
White crystals.

Uses
Potassium chloride is used as an essential nutrient and as a salt substitute.

Potassium as a nutrient lowers blood pressure, prevents bone loss, and reduces the risk of kidney stones. Some of these effects are due to the loss of sodium in the urine when potassium is ingested.

In salt substitutes, the metallic or bitter taste of potassium chloride is often masked by other ingredients, such as the amino acid L-lysine, tricalcium phosphate, citric acid, and glutamic acid.

Fats

9

Fats are food. But apart from their nutritive value they are also used as ingredients to modify other foods. Flaky piecrusts, smooth ice cream, and melt-in-your-mouth chocolates owe their properties to the unique characteristics of fats and oils.

Because fats are the most concentrated form of calories in foods, there are many reasons to try to attain those properties without all the calories. That's where vegetable gums and modified fats enter the picture.

Tristearin

Chemical Formula

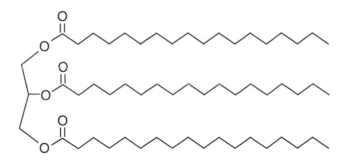

Synonyms
Glycerol tristearate

Description
White greasy solid.

Uses
Tristearin is the primary fat in beef. It is a triglyceride, a molecule of glycerin that has reacted with three molecules of the fatty acid stearic acid.

Tristearin is a saturated fat. This means that every carbon has as many hydrogen atoms as it can hold—it is saturated with hydrogen—and there are no double bonds between any two carbons. Carbon can form four bonds. If a carbon is attached to two other carbons in a chain, the atom has two bonds left that can attach to hydrogens.

Single bonds are flexible, and can bend and rotate easily. Double bonds are more rigid. A rigid bond does not allow the molecules to fit together easily, so they can't pack tightly into a solid.

Saturated fats are usually solid, while unsaturated fats or polyunsaturated fats (which have two or more double bonds) are usually liquid at room temperature.

Focus: Fats

Flaky piecrusts used to contain lard, or at least butter. Solid fats are important in baking, as they separate sheets of dough into thin, independent flakes.

Traditional solid fats are animal-derived saturated fats, such as lard and butter. Some vegetable fats, such as coconut and palm kernel oils, are solid, but they are more expensive than some liquid vegetable oils like corn oil, cottonseed oil, or soybean oil. These oils come from plants that are used for more than just the oil they provide. Using several different parts of the plant makes growing them more economical.

Saturated fats like the tristearin in beef fat have higher melting points than the unsaturated fats in vegetable oils like trilinolein or trilinolenin.

Shortening

Vegetable oils can be made into solids by converting some of the double bonds in their molecules into single bonds. This is done by adding hydrogen, and is called hydrogenation. A catalyst such as platinum is used to convert one or more double bonds to single bonds with an attached hydrogen. Some of the double bonds are converted from the normal *cis* orientation, with both hydrogens on the same side of the bond, to the *trans* orientation, with a hydrogen on either side of the bond. Such fats are called trans fats, and are implicated in cardiovascular problems. With the double bonds converted to single bonds, the molecules can fold and twist more easily, and the fat is now a solid.

Shortening also contains pieces of fats called monoglycerides and diglycerides. These are emulsifying agents that allow water and air to be whipped into the shortening and help to thicken it and make it gel.

Trilinolein

Chemical Formula

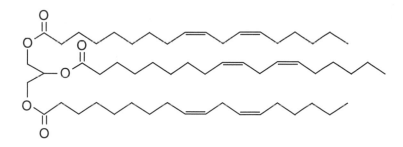

Synonyms
Glycerol trilinoleate

Description
Yellowish clear oil.

Uses
Trilinolein is a polyunsaturated fat. This type of fat is an antioxidant that has been linked to a number of potential cardiovascular health benefits. It is found in seed oils such as safflower oil and linseed oil.

The double bonds that make this an unsaturated fat prevent the molecule from bending; they lower the melting point making a liquid oil rather than a solid fat.

Polyunsaturated fats can combine easily with oxygen at the points where there is a double bond between two carbon atoms. This is why they make good antioxidants; they combine with the oxygen free radicals so they don't damage other molecules. It is also how oils harden, and is thus important to painters. Oil paints made with linseed oil are almost three-quarters trilinolein. They dry to form a tough plastic film that incorporates the pigments and holds them onto the surface to be painted.

Trilinolenin

Chemical Formula

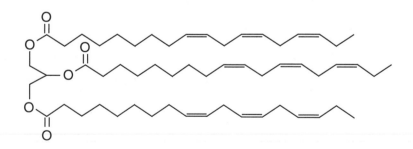

Synonyms
Glycerol trilinolenate

Description
Yellowish clear oil.

Uses

Trilinolenin is an omega-3 polyunsaturated fat. This type of fat, like trilineolin, has been linked to a number of beneficial health effects, and it is an antioxidant. It is found in oils such as soybean oil and linseed oil.

Omega-3 refers to a situation in which the first (or only) double bond is located on the fatty acid. The last carbon is called the omega carbon (omega is the last letter in the Greek alphabet). If there is a double bond between the third and fourth carbons from the end, the omega-3 and omega-4 carbons, then the oil is an omega-3 fat. Omega-3 fats are known for their beneficial cardiovascular effects.

Fat Substitutes

Olestra

Chemical Formula

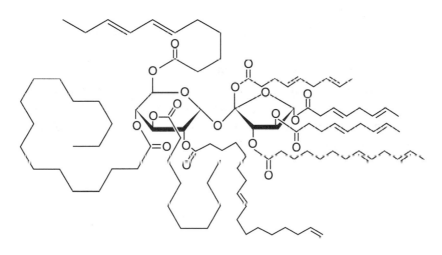

Synonyms
Sucrose octaester • sucrose polyester

Description
Amber medium-viscosity liquid.

Olestra is a nondigestible plastic, made by adding eight fatty acid molecules to the sugar molecule sucrose. The fatty acids block access to the sugar, so enzymes can't break it down. The result is a molecule that behaves like a fat, but cannot be digested by humans.

Because Olestra is not digested, it behaves much like mineral oil. The laxative properties, which are widely discussed, appear on the label. Like other indigestible lipids, Olestra can dissolve fat-soluble vitamins and carotenoids, which makes them unavailable for absorption.

Most users do not encounter problems. It is unclear at this time whether affected individuals cease to be affected over time, as they do with sorbitol and some other sugar alcohols that produce similar problems.

Olestra's manufacturing process creates many different molecules, some with fewer than eight fatty acids, and with many different fatty acid chains other than those pictured above.

Uses
Currently, Olestra is only approved for use in savory snacks, such as potato chips.

The molecules in Olestra have been modified since it was first marketed, to avoid some of the more unpopular side effects, but some remain. Adding carotenoids and fat-soluble vitamins to the product has also been done, but this does not eliminate all of the problems with nutrient absorption.

Salatrim

Chemical Formula

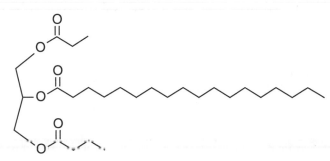

Synonyms
Structured triglyceride • Benefat

Description
Solid fat.

Salatrim is a mixture of many triglycerides that have the characteristics mentioned above. Because it is partially absorbed, Salatrim does not have the problems associated with Olestra. It does not have any laxative effects nor does it prevent the absorption of fat-soluble vitamins and carotenoids.

The available calories from Salatrim are only 55 percent of those from normal fats.

Uses
Salatrim is a fat (triglyceride), and can be used where fats are used in cooking. It is not as easily absorbed as other fats. This is because the main long-chain fatty acid in it is stearic acid, which by itself is less well absorbed than others, and because it is even less well absorbed when combined with short-chain organic acids like acetic (with two carbons), propionic (with three carbons), and butyric (with four carbons) acids. Short-chain organic acids have less energy storage capacity than long-chain fatty acids. The very short chains are closer to carbohydrates (in calories) than they are to fats.

Guar Gum

Chemical Formula

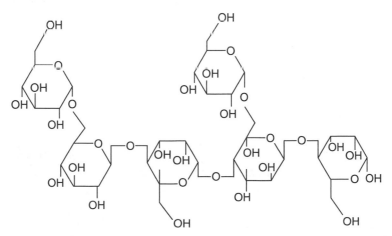

Description
Yellowish powder.

Guar gum is a polysaccharide (a long chain made of sugars) composed of the sugars galactose and mannose. Some other familiar polysaccharides are starch and cellulose, which are made of long chains of the sugar glucose.

Guar gum comes from the endosperm of the seed of the legume plant *Cyamopsis tetragonoloba*. *Cyamopsis tetragonoloba* is an annual plant, grown in arid regions of India as a food crop for animals.

Uses
Guar gum is used as a thickener in cosmetics, sauces, salad dressings; as an agent in ice cream to prevent ice crystals from forming; and as a fat substitute that adds the "mouth feel" of fat. In pastry fillings, it prevents syneresis (weeping of the water in the filling), keeping the pastry crust crisp.

It has a high viscosity (thickness) even when very little is used.

When mixed with xanthan gum or locust bean gum, the viscosity is more than when either one is used alone, so less of each can be used.

Focus: Ice Cream

 Ice cream is more American than apple pie. Thomas Jefferson made ice cream at Monticello. George Washington loved ice cream. It is said that ice cream is not food, it is medicine, capable of curing melancholy and lifting spirits, drowning sorrows, and bringing smiles to the most defeated of little soccer players.

Ice cream at its simplest is made of milk, sugar, cream, and some flavoring, such as fruit puree or vanilla. An essential ingredient in addition to those is air, without which ice cream would not be the special treat it is.

In the United States, ice cream must contain at least 10 percent milk fat, and at most 50 percent air, and must weigh at least

4.5 pounds per gallon. Ice creams labeled "premium" and "super premium" have higher fat content (13 to 17 percent) and lower air content (known in the ice cream trade as "overrun").

Ice Cream Ingredients

The milk and cream in ice cream contain butterfat, proteins, and milk sugars. Butterfat adds rich flavor, smooth texture, body, and good melting properties. The triglycerides in butterfat melt over a wide range of temperatures, so there is always some bit of solid and some liquid butterfat. Some of the butterfat almost turns into butter while the ice cream is being churned, adding to the unique texture of ice cream.

The proteins in ice cream help to incorporate air into the mixture; the air forms small bubbles. The proteins modify the texture of the ice cream in other ways as well, making it chewier and giving it body. The proteins also help to emulsify the fats, keeping the fat globules suspended in the mix. The proteins coat each fat globule and keep them from sticking together. However, making the globules stick together in chains and meshlike structures is important to ensuring the ice cream's texture, its ability to hold air, and its ability to stay firm as the ice inside melts. Emulsifiers, such as the lecithin in egg yolks, stick their fatty-acid ends into the fat globules and prevent the proteins from completely coating the fat. This balance between proteins and emulsifiers allows the fat globules to chain and stack without flowing together.

The milk sugar lowers the freezing point of the water in ice cream. Adding extra sweeteners, such as sugar and corn syrup, also has this effect. This ensures that a portion of the water never freezes, keeping the ice cream from becoming a solid chunk of ice. Added sweeteners are inexpensive, and they make up about 15 percent of the mix by weight. The use of high-fructose corn syrup will reduce the freezing point further than sugar, resulting in a softer ice cream.

Ice Cream Additives

As ice creams move down the scale from premium, getting lower in fat and incorporating more air, ingredients are added to make up for the loss of creamy texture—and to help keep all of the extra air whipped up.

Emulsifiers such as the monoglyceride glycerol monostearate and related diglycerides help to keep the milk fat in suspension, and limit the growth of ice crystals. Other emulsifiers such as lecithin and polysorbate 80 perform similar functions. Emulsifiers have a significant effect on making the fat globules stick together in chains, rather than flowing together in larger globules, or staying separated as tiny ones. This adds to the structure of the ice cream, as it affects the texture and the ability to incorporate air into the mixture.

Gums such as guar gum, locust bean gum, xanthan gum, carrageenan, and methylcellulose help to prevent ice crystals from forming during freezing and refreezing after a trip from the grocery store. They also have a "mouth feel" similar to milk fat, so the milk fat is not missed as much as it might be in low-fat ice creams. Like emulsifiers, gums also aid in keeping the air whipped into the mix. Gums keep the ice cream from becoming grainy due to crystals forming from either ice or lactose.

Some ice creams contain sodium citrate to decrease the tendency of fat globules to coalesce, and to decrease protein aggregation. This results in a wetter ice cream. The citrates and phosphates are both used for this effect. Calcium and magnesium salts have the opposite effect, making a dryer ice cream.

Other Icy Treats

Sherbet
Sherbets have a milk-fat content between 1 and 2 percent, and they usually contain more sugar. Often flavored with fruit, a gallon of sherbet weighs a minimum of six pounds.

> *Sorbet*
> Water ices and sorbets are similar to sherbet, but contain no dairy products.
>
> *Gelato*
> Gelato is made of sugar, milk, cream, egg yolks, and flavorings, and is usually served semifrozen.

Locust Bean Gum

Chemical Formula

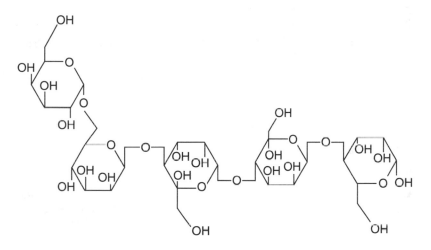

Synonyms
Carob bean gum

Description
Off-white powder.

Locust bean gum is a polysaccharide (a long chain made of sugars) made of the sugars galactose and mannose. Some other familiar polysaccharides are starch and cellulose, which are made of long chains of the sugar glucose.

In locust bean gum, the ratio of mannose to galactose is higher than in guar gum, giving it slightly different properties, and allowing the two gums to interact synergistically so that together they are able to make a thicker gel than either one would do alone.

Locust bean gum is extracted from the endosperm of the seeds of the carob tree, *Ceratonia siliqua*, which grows in Mediterranean countries.

Uses

The ancient Egyptians used locust bean gum to bind the wrapping of mummies.

In more recent times it is used as a thickener in salad dressings, cosmetics, and sauces; as an agent in ice cream that prevents ice crystals from forming; and as a fat substitute. In pastry fillings, it prevents syneresis (weeping of the water in the filling), keeping the pastry crust crisp.

It has a very high viscosity (thickness) even when very little is used.

Xanthan Gum

Chemical Formula
Xanthan gum is a long-chain polysaccharide composed of the sugars glucose, mannose, and glucuronic acid. The backbone is similar to cellulose, with added side chains of trisaccharides (three sugars in a chain).

Description

Creamy white crystalline powder.

A polysaccharide such as xanthan gum is a chain of sugars. Some familiar polysaccharides are starch and cellulose. The backbone of xanthan gum is similar to cellulose, but the trisaccharide side chains of mannose and glucuronic acid make the molecule rigid, and allow it to form a right-handed helix. These features make it interact with itself and with other long-chain molecules to form thick mixtures and gels in water.

Xanthan gum is a slimy gel produced by the bacterium *Xanthomonas campestris*, which causes black rot on cruciferous vegetables, such as cauliflower and broccoli. The slime protects the bacterium from viruses and prevents it from drying out.

Uses

Xanthan gum is used as a thickener in sauces, as an agent in ice cream that prevents ice crystals from forming, and as a fat substitute that adds the "mouth feel" of fat without the calories. It is used in canned pet food to add "cling." In pastry fillings, it prevents syneresis (weeping of the water in the filling), protecting the crispness of the crust.

It has a very high viscosity (thickness) even when very little is used.

When mixed with guar gum or locust bean gum, the viscosity is more than when either one is used alone, so less of each can be used.

Colors

10

Many foods and products become much more appealing if they have color. Margarine would look like vegetable shortening if it weren't for added color.

Some colors are nutrients in their own right, and they have antioxidant properties that are beneficial to health. Beta-carotene, annatto, saffron, and turmeric all have these good properties in addition to their color. In fact, the same chemistry that makes them absorb light also helps them to absorb and neutralize dangerous oxygen free radicals in the body.

Annatto

Chemical Formula

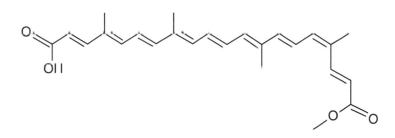

Bixin

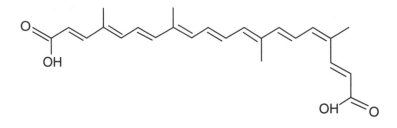

Norbixin

Synonyms
Bixin carotenoids

Description
Annatto is a colored pigment that is extracted from the Central and South American plant *Bixa orellana*. The color comes from the resinous outer covering of the seeds of the plant, which is composed of the carotenoid pigments bixin and norbixin and their esters. The central portion of those molecules is the same as that of the molecule beta-carotene, and the yellow-orange color of annatto comes from the same physical chemistry origins as the orange color of beta-carotene.

Uses
Annatto provides color in cheese, butter, margarine, and microwave popcorn. It is often used as a substitute for the expensive herb saffron. It also has antioxidant properties.

The seeds are used as a flavoring in the form of a powder or a paste, but the main use is as a coloring agent.

Because annatto binds well to the proteins in dairy foods, it is often used to add color to milk products such as butter, cheese, or puddings.

Beta-carotene

Chemical Formula

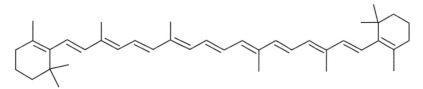

Synonyms
β-carotene

Description
Yellow powder.

Beta-carotene is one of the orange dyes found in most green leaves and in carrots. When leaves lose their chlorophyll in the fall, carotene is one of the colors left over in the leaf.

Uses
Beta-carotene is used in foods to provide color (margarine would look as white as vegetable shortening without it). Another similar molecule, annatto, is used in cheeses. Another famous carotenoid dye, saffron, is used to color rice and other foods.

Beta-carotene is sometimes added to products for its antioxidant effects, to keep fats from going rancid. The same long chains of conjugated double bonds (alternating single and double bonds) that give the carotenes their colors are also the reason they make good antioxidants. They can mop up oxygen free radicals and dissipate their energy.

The body turns beta-carotene into vitamin A, and it is sometimes added to foods or vitamin supplements as a nutrient.

Chemistry Lesson

Lycopene

Another colorful carotene is lycopene. This is the red molecule that gives ripe tomatoes their color.

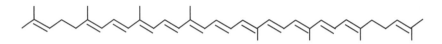

Notice the alternating double and single bonds between the carbon atoms. These are called conjugated bonds, or resonance bonds. The electrons in those bonds are not locked on to one atom—instead they spend their time bouncing from atom to atom. This gives the effect of something in between a double bond and a single bond, more of a one-and-a-half bond.

The long chain of conjugated bonds acts like a wire, allowing the electrical energy to move from one side of the molecule to the other. The energy can slosh around like water in a bathtub. Normally it takes quite a bit of energy to move an electron away from an atom. X-rays or high-energy ultraviolet light can move an electron into a higher orbit in an atom, but ordinary visible light does not have enough energy.

A molecule of lycopene can absorb blue light because the electrons are not orbiting a single atom, they are sloshing around orbiting many atoms, and the energy needed to move them is a lot less than in a smaller molecule, or one without conjugated bonds.

You can think of the energy in a lycopene molecule as a wave sloshing in a bathtub, or the wave you can make with a jump rope. The lowest energy state, called the ground state, would correspond to the jump rope going around in the normal fashion.

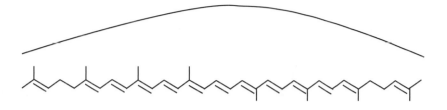

Each end of the jump rope is a node, a place where the rope doesn't move. It is possible to get a jump rope to have three nodes, as you may have done as a child. It acts like there are two jump ropes, each one half the length of the other. The energy sloshing around in the lycopene molecule can do the same thing. Absorbing a photon of green light makes it act as if the molecule were two molecules, each half as long.

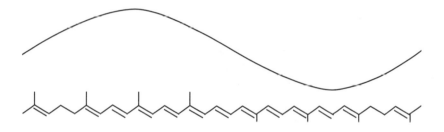

The molecule has absorbed the green light. White light that is missing its green light looks red. Beta-carotene absorbs blue light, so it looks orange.

Anthocyanins

Another class of colored compounds is the anthocyanins. Flowers, blueberries, apples, and red cabbage get their color from antho cyanins, which are part of a group of compounds known as flavenoids.

Anthocyanins can change their color, depending on how acidic or alkaline they are.

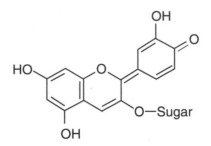

Cyanidin 3-glucoside

In neutral conditions, the molecule has no charge. It absorbs yellow light and appears purple. Notice all the alternating single and double bonds.

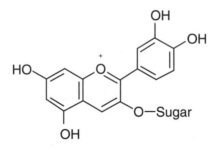

In an acid (pH less than 3), the acid donates a hydrogen nucleus, and the molecule becomes positive. The bond next to the oxygen becomes a double bond, and the molecule now absorbs green light, so it appears red.

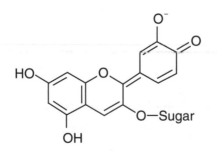

In an alkaline solution, the molecule donates a hydrogen nucleus, and a hydroxyl group becomes an oxygen atom with a negative charge. The molecule now absorbs orange light and appears blue.

You can try this yourself at home. You need some purple grape juice, blueberry juice, or the water left over after boiling a red cabbage. If you add clear distilled vinegar, the juice will turn red. If you add baking soda, the juice will turn blue.

You can learn more about molecules that absorb different colors in the section on para-amino benzoic acid (PABA).

Carmine

Chemical Formula

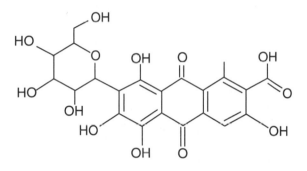

Synonyms
Cochineal extract • 7-D-glucopyranosyl-3,5,6,8-tetrahydroxy-1-methyl-9.10-dioxoanthracene-2-carboxylic acid

Description
Carmine is a colored pigment extracted from the female insect *Coccus cacti* or *Dactylopius coccus,* or its eggs. These insects live on prickly pear cactus in Mexico. The Spanish conquistador Hernán Cortés brought the dye to Europe after seeing the Aztecs use it.

It takes more than a million of the insects to make a pound of dye. The insects are harvested when the females are about to lay eggs, at which time they turn a bright red color. First, the shells of the female insects are dried; next, the color is dissolved in a solvent and all of the

excess insect parts are filtered out. Because of this labor-intensive processing, carmine is more expensive than FD&C Red #40. It has a deep
magenta color, while Red #40 is more of an orange-red.

Because carmine comes from insects, some other color must be
used if a product is to be labeled kosher.

Uses

Carmine (or cochineal) is used as a colorant in food, cosmetics, and
paints.

Carminic acid is orange in acidic media (pH 3), red in nearly neutral media (pH 5.5), and purple at pH 7. It forms complexes with metals such as tin and aluminum to make brilliant red pigments.

Carmine is easily bleached by sulfur dioxide.

Carminic acid is related to another dye molecule, alizarin.

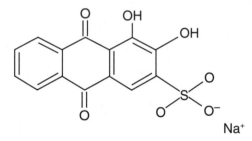

Alizarin 6

Also note the similarity to erythrosin B, known as FD&C Red #3:

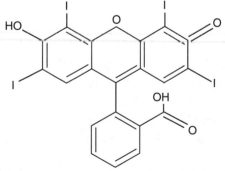

Erythrosin B

Focus: Food, Drug, and Cosmetic Colors

The term "FD&C color," often seen on ingredients labels, refers to food, drug, and cosmetic colors. These are organic compounds (as opposed to inorganic pigments, such as titanium dioxide) that are so intense in color that it takes only very tiny amounts to color something, and thus they can be used in concentrations so minute that they are safe for consumption.

As further described in the section on beta-carotene, organic dyes owe their colors to resonance structures in the molecule, where charges are free to move in the molecule at frequencies that fall in the range of visible light.

There are only seven non-natural (artificial) colors certified for consumption in the United States:

- FD&C Blue #1: Erioglaucine
- FD&C Blue #2: Indigotine
- FD&C Green #3: Fast Green
- FD&C Red #3: Erythrosin B
- FD&C Red #40: Allura Red
- FD&C Yellow #5: Tartrazine
- FD&C Yellow #6: Sunset Yellow

The dye Orange B is allowed only in hot dog and sausage casings.

Other FD&C colors are used in drug coatings and cosmetics.

If one of the above colors is used in a food product, it must be explicitly mentioned in the ingredients list. If the label does not name the compound specifically, but simply says something like "contains artificial color," then you know it does not contain one of the colors listed above.

A pigment is a solid that has a color. A dye is a liquid that has a color. FD&C colors are all dyes. To make a solid color from a dye, the dye is used to color a solid substance. The result is called a *lake*. One common substrate used is aluminum hydroxide, commonly used as an antacid. A color made this way might be labeled "Red 40 Aluminum Lake." Lakes are often used on the outside of candies and pills, so that the dye does not wash off or rub off.

Natural Colors

Besides artificial colors, many natural colors are used in foods. Some of these are:

- annatto
- beta-carotene
- carmine
- saffron
- turmeric
- indigo

Pigments such as titanium dioxide and ferrous gluconate are also added to foods.

Caramel Color

One of the most widely used colors is caramel, which is the color of burnt sugar. There are many different types of caramel color, each engineered to serve a particular purpose in food chemistry. They are all based on the cooking of sugars and starches. Sometimes acids such as acetic acid, citric acid, lactic acid, or phosphoric acid are used to break the bonds between sugars to create invert sugars, or to make sugars from starches, before the sugars are raised to a higher temperature for caramelization.

The heat is carefully controlled during caramelization to get the right products from the reaction. Besides acids, alkalies and salts may be used to further control the process.

Caramel color is a colloid, a mixture in which solid particles are suspended in water. The particles in colloids have electric charges that keep the particles from clumping together and settling out of solution. The charges can be positive or negative. If a negative colloid is added to a product that has positive colloidal particles in it, the two will attract one another and clump up, making the product cloudy.

Caramel color can be made with either positively or negatively charged particles. This allows manufacturers to use negative colloidal caramel in acidic soft drinks, and positive colloidal caramel in beers and soy sauces. Beer has positively charged proteins suspended in it, and soy sauce has a high salt content that requires the more salt-tolerant positive caramel color.

Caramel color is an emulsifying agent as well as a colorant. In soft drinks, it helps keep the flavor oils suspended in the solution.

In chocolate milk, the muddy color of caramel is darkened by the addition of FD&C Red #40 to give what the industry refers to as a Dutch chocolate shade. Blues and yellows are sometimes added to create a browner color.

Caramel color is added to baked goods, poultry, and milk (to give it an "eggnog" color), and to malt vinegars, canned meats, syrups, and soups, stews, and gravies.

Saffron

Chemical Formula

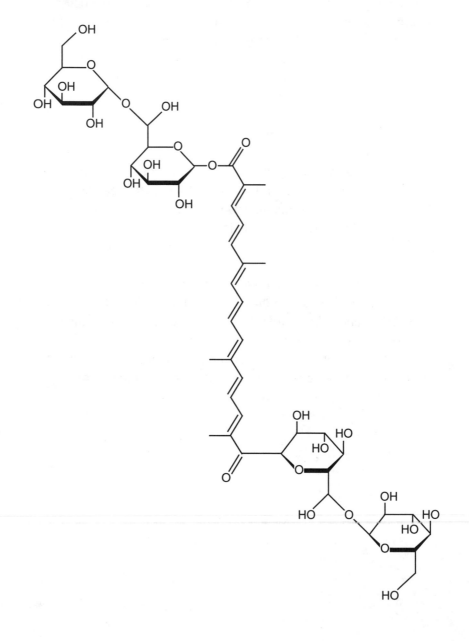

Synonyms
Beta-gentiobiose crocetin • saffron carotenoids

Description
Saffron is the tiny stigma at the center of the crocus flower, *Crocus sativus*. Because each stigma is plucked from the flower by hand, saffron is one of the most expensive spices in use today.

The dye molecule in saffron is the carotenoid beta-gentiobiose crocetin. It is related to beta-carotene, and you can see the relationship in the center of the molecule. That center portion is the carotenoid pigment crocetin:

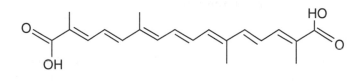

Crocetin

On either side of the crocetin molecule is a disaccharide molecule called beta-gentiobiose, and the result is the molecule that gives saffron its yellow color.

Uses
Saffron is a spice that is used sometimes for flavor, but mostly for the yellow color it imparts to foods. Because of its expense, saffron is often replaced in recipes by another carotenoid, annatto, or the unrelated dye molecule in turmeric. Like the other carotenoid dyes, saffron is an antioxidant, but its expense makes it unsuitable as a preservative or dietary supplement.

Turmeric

Chemical Formula

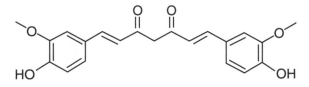

Synonyms
Curcumin

Description
Curcumin is the main color found in the root of the turmeric plant *Curcuma longa*, grown in south Asia.

Uses
Ground turmeric rhizome is one of the main ingredients in curry powder. Its bright yellow color makes it a natural substitute for the much more expensive herb saffron.

Because turmeric fades with exposure to light, other colors are necessary if a product is to be displayed in a clear container.

Titanium Dioxide

See entry, page 12.

Allura Red

Chemical Formula

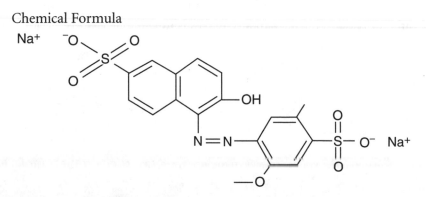

Synonyms
FD&C Red #40 • 6-hydroxy-5-(2-methoxy-5-methyl-4-sulfophenyl-azo)-2-naphtalenesulfonic acid sodium salt

Description
Red dye.

Uses
FD&C Red #40 is used as a coloring agent in a wide array of products, such as orange soda. It is related to several other dyes, including FD&C Yellow #6:

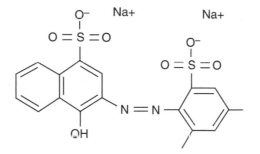

the food color Scarlet GN (FD&C Red #4):

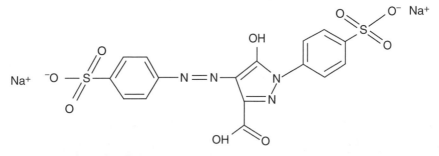

the food color tartrazine (FD&C Yellow #5):

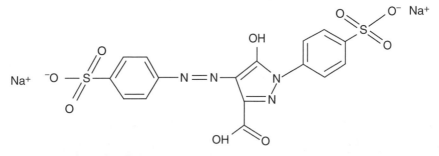

and the closely related dye Orange B:

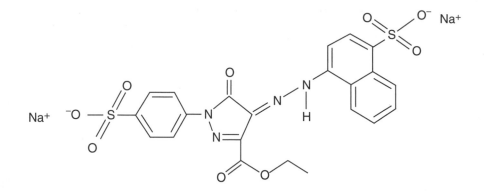

Yellow #5 and #6 are widely used in candies and drug coatings. Orange B is used in hot dog and sausage casings. Some people are sensitive to Yellow #5; reactions to it can be severe enough that specific labeling is required for prescription medicines that contain it. None of the other certified dyes have this special requirement.

 ## Chemistry Lesson

The dyes on the group above are known as azo dyes, because they have the two nitrogen atoms together in the center (called an azo group). These dyes were originally derived from coal tar, but are now mostly made from petroleum. Azo dyes come in many colors besides those allowed in food (listed above). The other colors find use in fabrics, paper products, and plastics.

Indigo

Chemical Formula

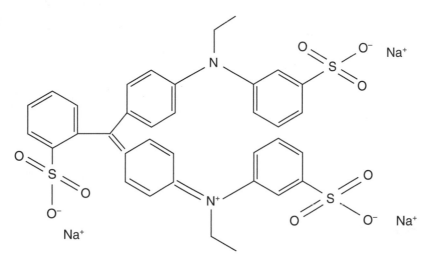

Synonyms
Indigotine • FD&C Blue #2

Description
Blue dye.

Indigo was originally made from two plants. One is woad, *Isatis tinctoria,* a native of Greece and Italy, and the other is indigo, *Indigofera tinctoria,* a native of India. At the end of the nineteenth century, German scientists synthesized the dye, and production from plant sources declined. Most of the dye today comes from China.

Recently, bacteria have been genetically engineered to produce Indigo dye.

Uses
Indigo is the dye used to color blue jeans. It is also used in foods under the name FD&C Blue #2. Other closely related dyes are erioglaucine, known as FD&C Blue #1:

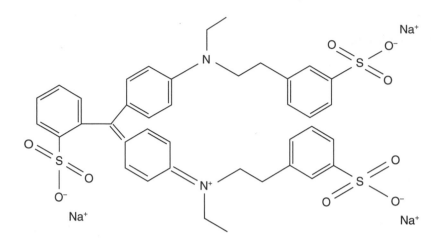

and Fast Green, FD&C Green #3:

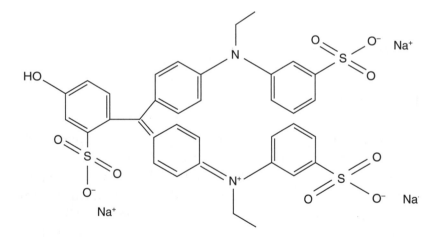

Caseinates

Chemical Formula
Casein proteins are composed of the following amino acids:

- 20.2 percent glutamic acid
- 10.2 percent proline
- 8.3 percent leucine*
- 7.4 percent lysine*

- 6.5 percent valine*
- 6.4 percent aspartic acid
- 5.7 percent serine
- 5.7 percent tyrosine
- 5.5 percent isoleucine*
- 4.5 percent phenylalanine*
- 4.4 percent threonine*
- 3.7 percent arginine
- 2.8 percent histidine
- 2.7 percent alanine
- 2.5 percent methionine*
- 2.4 percent glycine
- 1.1 percent tryptophan*
- 0.3 percent cystine

The amino acids marked with an asterisk are called essential amino acids, because they cannot be synthesized in the human body and must be obtained directly from food. All eight essential amino acids are present in casein protein.

Synonyms
Milk solids

Description
White powder.

Calcium caseinate is produced from skim milk by adding an acid to cause the protein to coagulate, at which point it can be filtered to separate the curds from the whey.

Sodium caseinate is produced by reacting the acid casein with sodium hydroxide.

Uses
Caseins are used in wine making to clarify the wine by causing fine particles to coagulate with the protein so they can be easily filtered out or precipitated.

In addition to their nutrient value, casein proteins have many other uses. They are good emulsifiers, helping fats to stay suspended in water-based products such as milkshakes, coffee creamers, and ice creams. They are used as binders in processed meats (lunch meats, sausages, etc.).

Caseinates are used as sources of nutritional protein.

Casein proteins were one of the first plastics, and they are still in use for this purpose. Thin plastic films of casein can be made by adding glycerol or sorbitol as a plasticizer, a substance that lowers the temperature at which a plastic softens, and makes it more pliable.

Caseins are used as food colorants because they make a nice base of opaque white, which can then be tinted with other colors as required.

Ferrous Gluconate

Chemical Formula

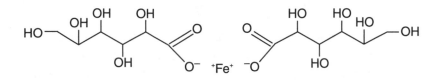

Synonyms
Iron (II) di-D-gluconate

Description
Ferrous gluconate is a black dye. It is composed of iron bound to two molecules of gluconic acid, which is the acid form of glucose.

Uses
Ferrous gluconate is the black dye used to color ripe olives. It is also used as an iron supplement to treat iron-deficiency anemia.

Moisture Controllers 11

Moisture controllers attract water. Sometimes they work so well that they actually pull water from the air. The liquid center of chocolate-covered cherries can be created by adding glycerin to the fondant that is molded around the cherry before it is dipped in chocolate. Over time, the glycerin absorbs so much water from the cherry that the fondant dissolves, making a liquid syrup inside the chocolate shell.

Glycerin

See entry, page 58.

Sorbitol

See entry, page 83.

Sodium PCA

Chemical Formula

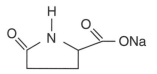

Synonyms
Sodium-2-pyrrolidone carboxylate

Description
Pale yellow clear liquid.

Uses
Sodium PCA is hygroscopic, attracting moisture from the air. It is used as a humectant (moisturizer) for hair- and skin-care products. It is a stronger hydrating agent than the traditional compounds used for this purpose, such as glycerin, propylene glycol, or sorbitol.

Mannitol

See entry, page 84.

Propylene Glycol

See Glycols entry, page 42.

Butylene Glycol

See Glycols entry, page 42.

Panthenol

Chemical Formula

Synonyms
Vitamin B5

Description
Off-white crystalline powder.

Panthenol is the alcohol form of pantothenic acid, more familiar as vitamin B5. In a living cell, panthenol is converted to pantothenic acid, which then becomes an important part of the compound coenzyme A, which is important in cellular metabolism. In hair, which contains no living cells, it remains panthenol.

Because it could become a vitamin if it were ever to get to a living cell, it is marketed as a "provitamin," even though its effects as a vitamin are never realized.

Uses
Because panthenol binds well to hair follicles and attracts moisture from the air, it is a moisturizing agent used in shampoos and conditioners. It lubricates the hair without feeling greasy. Instead, it smoothes roughened hair surfaces, making them shiny and easier to comb.

Contrary to advertising, panthenol does not nourish hair; instead it coats the hair and makes it slippery.

Emulsifiers

Emulsifiers are similar to detergents in that one end attracts water while the other attracts fats and oils. They are used to mix oil and water to make products such as mayonnaise, sauces, paints, and medicines.

Lecithin

See entry, page 20.

Phosphoric Acid

See entry, page 47.

Sorbitan Monostearate

Chemical Formula

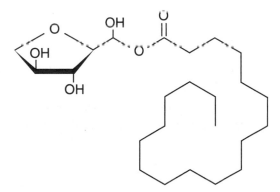

Synonyms
SPAN 60 • synthetic wax

Description
Waxlike creamy white powder.

Sorbitan monostearate is an ester of sorbitol and stearic acid. The sorbitol end of the molecule is highly soluble in water. The stearic acid end is soluble in fats. These properties allow the molecule to excel at making emulsions of oil and water.

Uses
Sorbitan monostearate is used as an emulsifying agent in cake mixes, icings, baked goods, puddings, imitation whipped cream, hemorrhoid creams, and creams to treat dry skin. It is often used with polysorbate 80.

Similar molecules can be made using other fatty acids, such as the shorter-chained lauric acid.

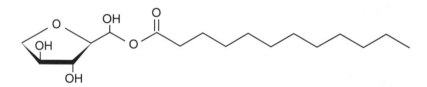

Sorbitan monolaurate

 Chemistry Lesson

An emulsion is a mixture of oil and water. Some emulsions, such as butter and margarine, have tiny droplets of water in the oil. Others, like cream or mayonnaise, are droplets of oil in water.

The choice of emulsifier has a large part to play in which kind of emulsion you get. Emulsifiers that are soluble in water generally have shorter chains of fats. These make emulsions of oil in water. Emulsifiers that have long-chain fats, or several chains, are more soluble in oil than they are in water. These make emulsions of water in oil.

The emulsifier polysorbate 80 is at the water-soluble end of the spectrum, making good emulsions of oil in water.

The emulsifier glycerol monostearate is closer to the oil-soluble end of the spectrum, making good emulsions of water in oil.

Somewhere in the middle are soy lecithin and sorbitan mono-laurate, which make good foam stabilizers in whipped cream and similar products.

Polysorbate 80

Chemical Formula

Synonyms
Polyoxyethylene sorbitan monooleate • (x)-sorbitan mono-9-octade-cenoate poly(oxy-1,2-ethanediyl)

Description
Amber-colored viscous liquid.

Uses
Polysorbate 80 is an emulsifying agent that is often used in ice cream to prevent milk proteins from completely coating the fat droplets. This allows them to join together in chains and nets, to hold air in the mixture, and to provide a firmer texture that holds its shape as the ice cream melts.

Similar compounds are polysorbate 60, polysorbate 65, etc.

Glycerol Monostearate

Chemical Formula
$CH_3(CH_2)_{16}COOCH_2CHOHCH_2OH$

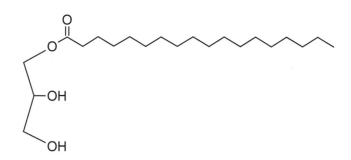

Synonyms
Glyceryl stearate • mono- and diglycerides • monostearin • octade-canoic acid monoester with 1,2,3-propanetriol

Description
White or cream-colored waxy solid.

Uses

Monoglycerides are used as emulsifying agents in many products, such as baked goods, whipped cream, and ice cream.

A monoglyceride is a fat that is missing two of its fatty acids. It is often used with diglycerides, which are fats that are only missing one of their fatty acids.

Tetrasodium Pyrophosphate

See entry, page 46.

Focus: Whipped Cream

The inventor of butter must have been an interesting person. What kind of person would shake a bunch of cream until his or her arms could shake no more, just to see what would happen? And who would keep going after the cream had whipped into the delight put on top of pies and sundaes for dessert?

Whipping cream is cream that contains at least 30 percent milk fat. Cream that has less than 30 percent fat will not whip. Heavy cream can contain up to 40 percent milk fat, and is sometimes used for whipping.

The structure of whipped cream is quite complex. A coating of milk protein surrounds small globules of milk fat containing both solid and liquid fats. These globules stack into chains and nets around air bubbles. The air bubbles are also formed from the milk proteins, which create a thin membrane around the air pockets. The three-dimensional network of joined fat globules and protein films stabilizes the foam, keeping the whipped cream stiff.

Whipped Cream Additives

Additives are sometimes added to whipping cream to make it easier to incorporate more air, or to make it more stable, so the foam lasts longer. Chief among the stabilizers are carrageenan and emulsifiers such as glycerol monostearate (a monoglyceride) and related compounds called diglycerides.

Carrageenan is a gelling agent that forms a complex with the milk proteins, adding bulk and strength. A small amount will make a large difference in the ability to hold air in the foam.

Mono- and diglycerides replace some of the proteins in the coating around the fat globules. This lets the globules partially fuse together to form the chains and networks that make up the three-dimensional structure of the foam. There are naturally occurring mono- and diglycerides in milk and cream, but adding more makes the whipped cream last longer and helps achieve higher volume.

Sweeteners such as sugar and corn syrup are added for taste, but they also participate in the structure of the foam and in the weight of the final product.

Natural and artificial flavors are also added, usually in the form of vanilla extract or synthetic vanillin or ethyl vanillin.

Propellant in Canned Whipping Cream

In canned whipping cream, the gas nitrous oxide is used as both a propellant and a whipping agent. Nitrous oxide under pressure dissolves in the fats in the cream, and comes out of solution (like fizzing carbon dioxide in a soda) when the pressure is released. The bubbles of nitrous oxide instantly whip the cream into foam.

Stabilizers and Thickeners

Stabilizers work with emulsifiers to prevent the fats and oils from separating. They can be emulsifiers themselves, or they can be large molecules, such as vegetable gums, that lock up the water in gels.

Corn Syrup

See Sugars entry, page 29.

Sodium Caseinate

See Caseinates entry, page 122.

Calcium Caseinate

See Caseinates entry, page 122.

Polyethylene Glycol

Chemical Formula

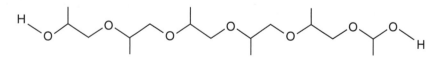

Synonyms
PEG-*n*: PEG-6, PEG-8, PEG-12, PEG-40, PEG-150, etc.

Description
Polyethylene glycol is a family of long-chain polymers attached to a glycerin backbone.

Uses
PEG is used as a thickener in many products. It is used in toothpaste to prevent bacteria from breaking down the pyrophosphates that control tartar buildup.

PEGs are often reacted with fatty acids to make detergents that have thickening and foam-stabilizing properties. When chemically combined with fatty acids from coconut oil, they make detergents such as PEG-5 cocamide, which is used in shampoos as a surfactant, emulsifier, and foam stabilizer.

Polypropylene Glycol

Chemical Formula

Synonyms
PPG-*n*: PPG-6, PPG-8, PPG-12, PPG-40, PPG-150, etc. • PPG-166/66 copolymer

Description
Polypropylene glycol is a family of long-chain polymers attached to a glycerin backbone.

Uses

Like the closely related compound polyethylene glycol, PPG is used as a thickener in many products. It is used in toothpaste to prevent bacteria from breaking down the pyrophosphates that control tartar buildup.

Lecithin

See entry, page 20.

Methylcellulose
Sodium Carboxymethylcellulose

Chemical Formula

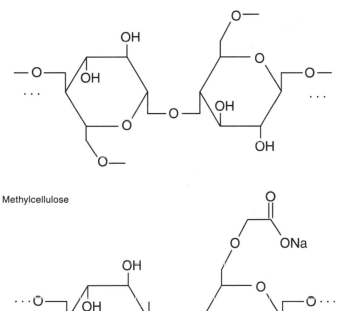

Methylcellulose

Sodium carboxymethylcellulose

Synonyms
Hydroxymethylcellulose • carboxymethylcellulose

Description
Methylcellulose and carboxymethylcellulose are forms of the familiar polysaccharide cellulose that have been treated to make them more soluble in water. Cellulose is a long chain made of the sugar glucose. The long chains mix with water to create a thick syrup or gel.

Uses
Methylcellulose is used as a thickener in sauces and salad dressings, and as a thickener and stabilizer in ice cream, where it helps prevent ice crystals from forming during freezing or during refreezing after a thaw.

Xylenesulfonates

Chemical Formula

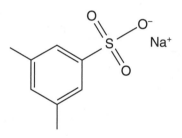

Synonyms
Ammonium xylenesulfonate • sodium xylenesulfonate • sodium dimethylbenzenesulfonate

Description
Sodium xylenesulfonate (or its ammonium cousin) are *hydrotropes*—organic compounds that increase the ability of water to dissolve other molecules.

Uses

Xylenesulfonates are used in detergents and shampoos in amounts of up to 10 percent of the product.

They are surfactants, but they are usually added to thicken mixtures such as shampoo, and to help keep some other ingredients in solution. This makes the product transparent, as the cloudy precipitates are put back into solution.

Agar

Chemical Formula

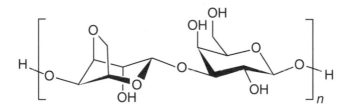

Synonyms
Seaweed extract

Description
Agar is made up of two polysaccharides, agaropectin and agarose. As with carrageenan, the backbone of these polysaccharides is the sugar galactose.

Uses
Agar is most familiar as the gelatinous growth medium used in petri dishes to culture bacteria. But it is also used in cooking as a gel for jellies and fillings. It is a soluble fiber, and as such it is quite useful as a laxative and diet aid.

As a growth medium, agar has nice properties, such as a high melting point (85°C), and a lower solidifying point (40°C). It can stay gelled at incubating temperatures. Purified agarose is used as a medium for electrophoresis, the separation of proteins or DNA fragments by size using an electric field.

Gelatin

Chemical Formula

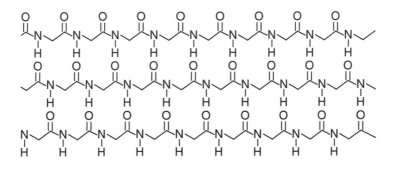

Synonyms
Bone and skin extract • collagen

Description
White powder.

Gelatin is a protein, made from the hydrolysis of collagen, a protein that makes up about a third of all mammalian tissue. Collagen is a key component of connective tissues, tendons, and bones.

Hydrolysis in proteins is the process of adding a molecule of water to break the bonds between some of the amino acids, thereby making the protein chains smaller.

Collagen forms a triple helix, where three chains of connected amino acids form weak hydrogen bonds between the double-bonded oxygen atoms and the hydrogen atoms attached to the adjacent chain's nitrogens. The three chains then twist together like three cords in a rope.

In gelatin, when the triple helixes are heated in water, they open up. Some of the hydrolyzed ends fray out to tangle with other ropes, and water is trapped in the strands. The result is a gel, a wiggly semi-solid mass.

Uses

Gelatin is very familiar as the gelling agent in Jell-O desserts. It is also used to thicken yogurt, sour cream, and ice creams. In its dried form it is used to make the dissolvable capsules that make medicines easier to swallow.

In its unrefined form, gelatin is the hide glue used to hold violins together.

Gelatin is the binder that makes marshmallows possible. It's also the ingredient that gives gummi bears their gumminess.

Pectin

Chemical Formula

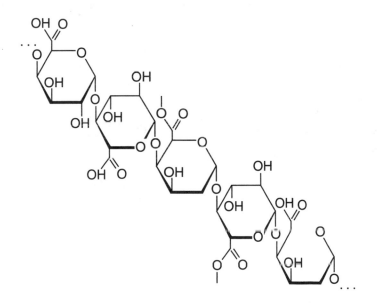

Synonyms
Heterosaccharide gel • homogalacturonan

Description

Viscous, slightly milky liquid.

Pectin is a long chain of pectic acid and pectinic acid molecules. Because these acids are sugars, pectin is categorized as a polysaccharide. It is prepared from citrus peels and the remains of apples after they are squeezed for juice. In the plant, pectin is the material that joins the plant cells together. When fungus enzymes break down the pectin in fruit, the fruit gets soft and mushy.

Uses

Pectin is a thickener in many products. If there is sufficient sugar in the mixture, pectin forms a firm gel. Jams and jellies are thickened with pectin. Pectin binds water, and thus keeps products from drying out. It stabilizes emulsions.

Pectin combines with the calcium and whey proteins of milk, stabilizing foams and gels made with cream or milk.

Pectin is not digested, and it is considered a beneficial dietary fiber.

Alginates

Chemical Formula

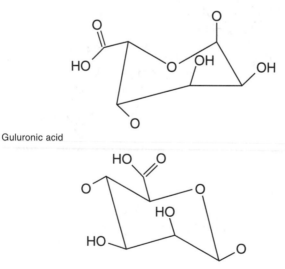

Guluronic acid

Mannuronic acid

Synonyms
Kelp extract • furcellaran

Description
White powder.

Alginates are made up of long chains of two monomers: guluronic acid and mannuronic acid. The chains can be made of all one monomer or mixtures of both. The stems of kelp are made of chains with more guluronic acid, and the leaves (fronds) have more mannuronic acid. Guluronic chains bind tightly to calcium; in mannuronic chains the calcium is more easily replaced by sodium, allowing the fibers to swell easily.

Uses
As with carrageenan, another seaweed extract, the ability to bind to calcium makes alginates useful in dairy products as a thickener. It also makes alginates useful as wound dressings, where they absorb fluids, and stop bleeding, and act as a scaffold.

Alginates are used as thickeners in fat substitutes, pet food, stuffed olives, onion rings, low-fat sauces and spreads, and pie fillings.

Propylene glycol alginate is stable in acids. It is used to preserve the foamy head on beers.

Starch and Modified Starch

Chemical Formula

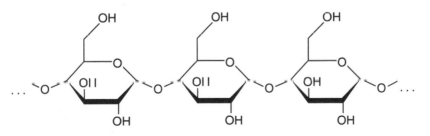

Amylose

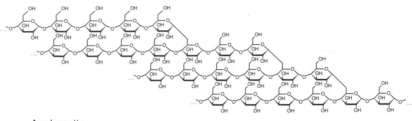

Amylopectin

Synonyms
Corn starch • polysaccharide • complex carbohydrate

Description
White powder.

Starch is a polysaccharide, a chain of many glucose molecules. It is the main carbohydrate store in roots and seeds.

There are two types of glucose chains in starch. One is a simple chain called amylose, and the other is a complex branched form called amylopectin. In the starch grains in a plant, amylopectin makes up the bulk of the material, from 50 to 80 percent by weight, made up of several million amylopectin molecules per starch grain. The rest is a much larger number of the smaller amylose chains, made up of 500 to 20,000 glucose units in each chain. Amylopectin molecules are made of several million glucose units.

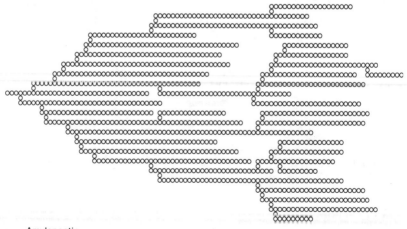

Amylopectin

Amylopectin forms branched structures with about 30 glucose units in a chain between branches. This makes the molecule somewhat striped in appearance, with the knotted branch points all in a row, and the smooth chains separating them. These molecules are so large that this striped appearance shows up under a light microscope, forming what appear to be growth rings in the starch grain.

Uses

Starch is a major source of calories in grains and tubers and foods made from them.

When starch is added to products as an ingredient, however, it is the functional properties of the starch that are usually important, not the calories.

Starch is the main thickener in gravies, sauces, and puddings. It absorbs water, and becomes a gel when cooked. As the starch swells up with water, the amylose leaches out, and the amylopectin forms the gel. Some starches have higher amylopectin content and make better gels than those containing large amounts of amylose.

As a thickener (as opposed to a gel), it is amylose that has the main function. The long water-soluble chains increase the viscosity, which doesn't change much with temperature. Amylose chains tend to curl up into helixes (spirals) with the hydrophobic parts inside. This allows them to trap oils, fats, and aroma molecules inside the helix.

Because starches are so good at absorbing water and bulking up, they are important in the texture of many food products. They are often used as fat substitutes.

Not all of the starch in a food ends up being digested. The starch that is not absorbed by the body is called resistant starch, and it is considered dietary fiber. It is also a source of nutrition for intestinal flora, which make important vitamins (and intestinal gas).

Starches are added to processed meats—lunch meats, hot dogs, sausages, etc.—as fillers, binders, moisture retainers, and fat substitutes. They are added to soups, sauces, and gravies as thickeners. They are used in extruded cereals and snacks to hold the shape of the material.

Modified Starch

Starches can be modified in several ways to change their function as additives. They can be cross-linked, where the chains get stuck together into a mesh. They can be heated to break the long chains down into simpler molecules like dextrin, polydextrin, and maltodextrin. These are simply short starches.

Starches can have a hydrogen replaced by something else, such as a carboxymethyl group, making carboxymethyl starch.

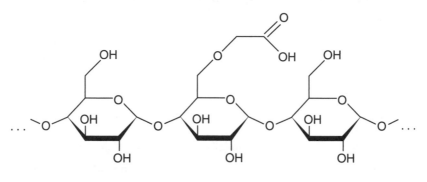

Carboxymethyl starch

Adding the carboxymethyl group makes the starch less prone to damage by heat and bacteria. Carboxymethyl starch is used as an additive in oil drilling mud. It is also used in the goo that makes ultrasound examinations so messy. Carboxymethyl starch is also called a starch ether.

Carboxymethyl groups make the starch more hydrophilic (water-loving), and aid in cross-linking. This makes carboxymethyl starch useful in aspirin and other tablets to make them disintegrate quickly.

Longer carbon chains can also be added, such as carboxyethyl groups, or carboxypropyl groups. Adding bulky functional components like carboxymethyl and carboxyethyl groups reduces the tendency of the starch to recrystallize. When the starch stays as a gel, a product is softer, and we refer to it as fresh. When the starch regains its crystalline form, the product becomes firmer, and we refer to it as stale. The technical term for this recrystallization is *starch retrogradation.*

Starches can be esterified by modifications with an acid. An ester is the result of reacting an alcohol with an acid. The starch loses a hydroxyl group, and the acid loses a hydrogen. These combine to form water as the other product of the reaction.

Using acetic acid, starch acetates are formed, which are used as film-forming polymers for pharmaceutical products, and as the polymer in biodegradable packing-foam peanuts. Starch acetates have a lower tendency to create gels than unmodified starch.

Acids can also break the long chains into shorter molecules, much as heat does, to form polydextrins, maltodextrin, or dextrin. Enzymes are used to do the same thing.

Cross-linking occurs when a hydroxyl group (OH) on one chain bonds with a hydroxyl group on an adjacent chain. This toughens the starch and helps it resist heat and acids. Cross-linking can be done by heating, or by reacting with compounds such as phosphates or glycerol.

Starches are also sometimes *pregelatinized* to make them easier to dissolve during product manufacture.

Starches, especially modified starches, are also used as glues in cardboard manufacturing. Starches such as gum arabic and gum tragacanth are used as the glue for stamps and postal envelopes.

Oxidized starch, usually oxidized with sodium hypochlorite, is whiter than unmodified starch; it has increased clarity and lower viscosity.

Carrageenan

Chemical Formula

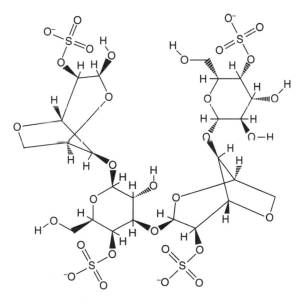

Synonyms
Seaweed extract

Description
White powder.

Carrageenan is a long-chain polysaccharide with a backbone of the sugar galactose.

Uses
Carrageenan is widely used in dairy products because it forms complexes with calcium and milk proteins. It thickens and helps suspend cocoa particles in chocolate milk. It stabilizes ice cream to protect it from thawing and refreezing, and enables it to hold more air.

It is used as a thickener in flans, custards, and puddings. It helps to keep whipped toppings foamy, and it thickens diet shakes and instant breakfast drinks.

It is also used as a dough conditioner in breads and pastries.

Guar Gum

See entry, page 97.

Locust Bean Gum

See entry, page 101.

Brominated Vegetable Oil

Chemical Formula

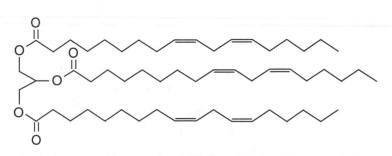

Synonyms
BVO

Description
Dense, oily liquid.

Uses
Brominated vegetable oil is ordinary oil, such as olive oil, that has had bromine added at various places to give the molecule the density of the sugar water in soft drinks. This allows BVO to keep citrus and other oil-based flavorings in solution without separating into an oil layer floating on top of the beverage. The result is the cloudy solution you see in orange-flavored or grapefruit-flavored soft drinks.

The chemical formula depicted above is that of trilinolein, a representative component of vegetable oils. Bromine atoms attach at various places on the molecule to form BVO. The amount of bromine is controlled to produce the desired density.

Gum Arabic

Chemical Formula
Polysaccharides and glycoprotein complex

Synonyms
Gum acacia • gum tragacanth (a similar gum) • gum karaya (also a similar gum) • gum ghatti (also a similar gum)

Description
White powder

Gum arabic is a complicated mixture of long and short chains of sugars (arabinogalactan oligosaccharides and polysaccharides) and glycoproteins (proteins with sugars attached). It is a powder that becomes a sticky glue or gum when mixed with water. It is extracted from the sap of the *Acacia senegal* and *Acacia seyal* trees native to the Sahara desert.

Uses

Gum arabic (gum acacia) is used as the lickable glue on stamps and envelopes, and as a flavor stabilizer (emulsifier) in soft drinks. It has components that bind to water, and components that bind to oils, making it an emulsifier but not a surfactant (because of the high molecular weight).

It is used in hard candies and as a foam stabilizer in marshmallows.

The similar products gum tragacanth, gum karaya, and gum ghatti are used in much the same way—as acid-resistant thickeners in sauces and salad dressings.

Xanthan Gum

See entry, page 102.

Dough Conditioners and Whipping Agents

14

What could be simpler than bread? Flour, water, salt, and yeast are all you need, right? But if you want to ship the bread across the country, store it on shelves for a while, and avoid having it go stale or moldy, you might want to consider getting a little help from some other foods and food products.

Most of the long, scary-sounding chemicals listed on packages of supermarket bread are actually made from other foods; they are added to prevent the starch in the bread from changing, oxidizing, or becoming moldy.

Sodium Stearoyl Lactylate

Description

Off-white power.

Sodium stearoyl lactylate (and the similar calcium stearoyl lactylate) is made by combining lactic acid and stearic acid, and then reacting the result with sodium hydroxide or calcium hydroxide to make the sodium or calcium salt.

Replacing the lactic acid with fumaric acid gives sodium stearoyl fumarate, a compound with the same uses as the other two.

Uses

Sodium stearoyl lactylate is an emulsifier that is used as a dough strengthener in baked goods. It has several features that combine to make it very popular with bakers. It maintains the texture of freshly baked bread by keeping the amylose starch in its gelled state and preventing its recrystallization. It makes the gluten in the bread stronger and more extensible, increasing the volume of the loaf. It disperses the fats in the bread, making it softer, which means less fat is needed. It absorbs water, allowing the baker to get 1 to 1.5 percent more loaves from the same ingredients, thus making each loaf less expensive to manufacture. Finally, it has a sweet taste, which means less sugar is needed.

Calcium Stearoyl Lactylate

See Sodium Stearoyl Lactylate entry, page 151.

Sodium Stearoyl Fumarate

See Sodium Stearoyl Lactylate entry, page 151.

Focus: Bread

The smell of a home-baked loaf, the taste of a flaky crescent, the texture of a slice of whole-grain bread— all these experiences can come from very basic ingredients. The simplest breads are made from flour, water, yeast, and salt. This is fine for breads that are eaten the same day they are baked.

Things get a little more complicated when the bread is required to last for days without going stale, to be inexpensive, and to be consistent at any time of the year with grain from any supplier.

Wheat flour contains starch and protein, which form the structure of the bread. Two of the proteins in flour, gliadin and the enzyme glutenin, form the elastic protein gluten when water is added and the mixture is stirred. Kneading the bread stretches the gluten into elastic sheets that can fill with gas to form bubbles, making the bread lighter in texture. Yeast supplies the gas. Yeast feeds on sugars in the flour and produces carbon dioxide gas and alcohol as waste products.

The final ingredient, salt, is added to slow down the rate of fermentation of the yeast. This gives a baker a certain amount of control over the rising process, ensuring that the bread will have the desired texture and will cook evenly.

Flour

Wheat flour can be made from whole wheat, or the germ and bran can be separated from the endosperm, which is then ground into flour. Without the fibrous bran and the oily germ, the resulting flour has fewer nutrients. However, it will create a lighter-textured, higher-rising bread that will keep longer.

If flour is allowed to age for about a month, its natural yellowish color will fade to white due to the effects of oxygen. This aging period can allow insects to spoil the flour, and is often eliminated by adding bleaching agents, such as benzoyl peroxide.

Malted barley flour is often added to bread because it gives the yeast more nutrients—primarily sugars—and gives the bread a different taste. Malting a grain is the process of letting the grain soak in water until it starts to sprout. The young sprouting barley plant converts some of the starch in the barley endosperm into sugars. The barley is then cooked or ground into flour, which stops the sprout from eating the sugars, leaving them available to the yeast. Sometimes sugar or high-fructose corn syrup is added as a yeast nutrient, or to make the crust of the bread brown more easily.

Some breads contain flour made from soybeans, which gives them added protein and a different texture. Soy flour absorbs water to make a gel, making the bread denser.

Some of the nutrients lost when the wheat germ and bran are discarded are returned to the flour by adding small amounts of vitamins and minerals. Among the nutrients most commonly added are niacin, thiamine, riboflavin, folic acid, iron, and calcium.

Vegetable oils are added to breads to shorten the strands of gluten and give the bread a more cakelike texture. Adding fats or oils also keeps bread from getting stale, which allows for storage of longer than one day.

How Bread Gets Stale

Stale bread tastes and feels dry, even though the moisture content is actually the same as in fresh bread. The recrystallization of the starch in bread is what makes it go stale. To combat this, fats and oils are added to bread to form a complex with the starch in its gelled form, slowing down the recrystallization process and keeping the starch in its flexible gel form.

Fats and oils, however, interfere with gluten, making the gluten strands shorter and thus preventing the loaf from increasing in volume. So emulsifiers are commonly used instead of fats to control staling. Emulsifiers have a fatty acid at one end that combines with the starch, as well as a water-loving end that helps to keep the starch dispersed in the dough. Emulsifiers aid in distributing fats and oils throughout dough, so less fat or oil is needed.

Some emulsifiers commonly used in baked goods are:

- lecithin
- sodium stearoyl lactylate
- glycerol monostearate
- diglycerides

Another way to prevent bread from becoming stale is to add humectant (water-attracting) agents to the dough. To recrystallize, starch needs water. By attracting water away from the starch, humectants keep it from recrystallizing and at the same time add more moisture to the product. Moist bread tastes better and has better texture, and it weighs more without adding expensive ingredients. Thus, a one-pound loaf of bread with higher water content is less expensive than a drier one-pound loaf.

Salt and sugar are good humectants. Sugars that are less sweet, such as dextrose (glucose), have excellent humectant properties.

Dough Conditioners

Bakers often use additives to change the dough in certain ways and give themselves more control over the baking process. Some of these dough conditioners are:

- sodium stearoyl lactylate
- calcium dioxide
- calcium iodate
- potassium iodate
- ammonium sulfate (yeast nutrient)
- potassium persulfate (strong oxidizer used as a strengthening agent)
- ammonium persulfate (strong oxidizer used as a strengthening agent)
- calcium sulfate
- ascorbic acid
- amylase
- azodicarbonamide
- calcium propionate

Potassium Bromate

Chemical Formula
$KBrO_3$

Synonyms
Bromated flour • bromic acid • potassium salt

Description
White crystals or powder.

Uses
Potassium bromate is used as a flour improver. It strengthens the dough to allow for higher rising. It is an oxidizing agent, and under the right conditions it will be completely used up in the baking bread. However, if too much is used, or if the bread is not cooked long enough or at a high enough temperature, then a residual amount will remain.

Potassium bromate has been banned in several countries as a carcinogen.

Carrageenan

See entry, page 147.

Tetrasodium Pyrophosphate

See entry, page 46.

Fumaric Acid

See entry, page 66.

Stimulants

15

At one time, Coca-Cola actually contained a form of cocaine. These days, the primary stimulant in Coca-Cola and many other beverages is caffeine. Other stimulants are less obvious. Chocolate contains theobromine, a caffeinelike stimulant. Nondrowsy cold remedies contain pseudoephedrine, a relative of ephedra, another plant-alkaloid stimulant.

Caffeine

Chemical Formula

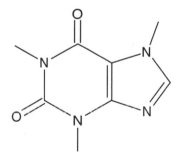

Synonyms
Trimethylxanthine

Description
White crystalline powder with a bitter taste.

Uses
Caffeine is an addictive drug used in soft drinks as a stimulant. It occurs naturally in coffee, tea, and chocolate.

It is added to pain relievers because it enhances the effects of aspirin and because many headaches are caused by caffeine withdrawal. Caffeine closes down blood vessels by competing with adenosine, and helps alleviate the vascular headaches caused by withdrawal.

A cup of drip-brewed coffee typically contains 100 milligrams of caffeine per 177 milliliters (6 ounces). Tea has about 70 milligrams, and colas have about 50 milligrams. A bar of milk chocolate has about 36 milligrams in 177 milliliters.

Caffeine binds to adenosine receptors in the brain, preventing adenosine from inducing sleep or opening blood vessels. Caffeine also increases levels of dopamine, the neurotransmitter associated with pleasure. This is the chemical mechanism for addiction. The response to adenosine competition causes increased adrenaline flow.

Theobromine

Chemical Formula

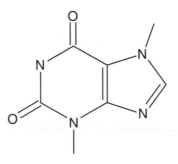

Synonyms
Dimethylxanthine • 3,7-dihydro-3,7-dimethyl-1H-purine-2,6-dione

Description
White crystalline powder with a bitter taste.

Uses
Theobromine is related to caffeine, but it has different effects in the body and brain. It is the mood-enhancing drug in chocolate. It is also the ingredient in chocolate that is toxic to dogs.

The name *theobromine* means "food of the gods."

Ephedrine

Chemical Formula

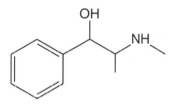

Synonyms
Pseudoephedrine • ma huang • ephedra • Mormon tea

Description
Ephedrine is the principal active ingredient in the herb ephedra, or ma huang. It is similar in form to the appetite-control drug phenyl-propanolamine (banned in the United States), which is also known as norephedrine, meaning ephedrine whose methyl group has been replaced by a hydrogen.

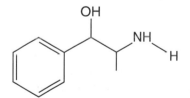

Phenylpropanolamine (norephedrine)

It is also similar to the controlled stimulant amphetamine, which is norephedrine with the hydroxyl group replaced by a hydrogen.

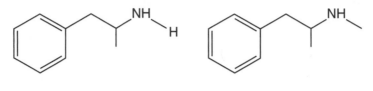

Amphetamine   Methamphetamine

Pseudoephedrine is an isomer of ephedrine in which the hydroxyl group is on the other side of the molecule.

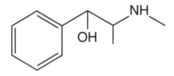

Pseudoephedrine

Uses

Ephedra is used in diet products as an appetite depressant and stimulant, and in sports drinks to mask fatigue. It is also used as a bronchial stimulator, and to relieve symptoms of the common cold.

Ephedrine enhances the release of the hormone norepinephrine in the body, and also binds to the same receptors as that hormone, causing excess calories to be converted to heat instead of being stored as fat. It also raises blood pressure. Epinephrine and norepinephrine are also known as adrenaline and noradrenaline. Ephedrine thus acts to stimulate an adrenaline rush.

Interactions with caffeine and aspirin can increase the effects of ephedrine. Norepinephrine works in part by increasing the levels of cyclic aminomethyl propanol (AMP) in cells. Caffeine inhibits the enzyme that breaks down cyclic AMP. Together, ephedrine makes more cyclic AMP, and caffeine prevents it from breaking down. Aspirin inhibits the receptors that turn off release of norepinephrine.

So ephedrine releases norepinephrine, and aspirin prevents the release from being turned off.

Ephedrine by itself has been shown to be ineffective as a weight-loss treatment. Ephedrine combined with either caffeine or aspirin is effective. The effect appears to stem from a combination of appetite reduction and avoidance of the metabolic rate decrease usually associated with a reduced-calorie diet.

Due to its effect as a stimulant on the heart and central nervous system, ephedrine can cause heart problems, stroke, and other medical complications (including death). For this reason, there has been pressure to regulate or ban it in the United States, as was done with similar drugs.

Medicines

16

We take aspirin to relieve pain, and sometimes to eliminate the cause of the pain, such as inflammation, fever, or joint swelling. We put germ killers on our skin, and we swallow pills to kill germs inside us. The chemistry of how these ingredients work in or on our bodies is the business of huge industries and large amounts of research.

Benzoyl Peroxide

Chemical Formula
$(C_6H_5CO)_2O_2$

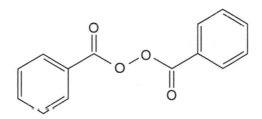

Description
White or off-white needle-shaped water-soluble crystals.

Uses
Benzoyl peroxide is used as a bleaching agent in wheat flour, but its more familiar use is as a powerful acne medication that can lay claim to the following benefits:

- Like salicylic acid and resorcinol, it causes dead skin cells to slough off.
- It kills the *Propionibacterium acnes* bacterium that causes acne pimples.
- It has an anti-inflammatory effect that reduces pimples and the pain they cause.
- It is a bleaching agent that oxidizes dyes to make them colorless.
- It eliminates fatty acids on the skin.

Chemistry Lesson

A peroxide is a compound that has an oxygen-oxygen bond. That is, it has two oxygen atoms bound together. Look again at the structural formula above. The molecule is symmetrical, with two identical parts joined at their oxygen atoms with an oxygen-oxygen bond.

A familiar peroxide is hydrogen peroxide. It has two oxygen atoms bound together, and each of those atoms in turn bind it to a hydrogen atom.

Peroxides make good bleaches. The oxygen atoms combine with dyes to make the dyes colorless. This process, called *oxidation*, can kill germs.

Focus: Acne Medicines

Acne is caused when skin cells shed too quickly in hair follicles. This clogs the follicle, producing comedones, more commonly known as whiteheads and blackheads. These can then become inflamed and turn into pimples.

Acne medicines may contain ingredients such as salicylic acid, benzoyl peroxide, and sulfur, which remove the top layer of dead skin. They may also contain ingredients that have antibacterial action. Some ingredients reduce sebum production; others reduce inflammation.

Sulfur

Sulfur was once quite common in acne medications, but while it was effective at reducing inflammatory lesions, it caused more whiteheads and blackheads, from which the inflammatory lesions form. For this reason, it is usually combined with something like salicylic acid, or resorcinol, to eliminate the comedones.

Resorcinol

Resorcinol unclogs pores by causing dead skin cells to slough off. It also has antifungal and antibacterial effects.

Benzoyl Peroxide

Benzoyl peroxide can help remove dead skin cells, which in turn prevents the pores from clogging up. It also kills the *Propionibacterium acnes* bacterium that causes acne. It has anti-inflammatory effects and reduces oxygen free radicals and fatty acids on the skin.

Salicylic Acid

Salicylic acid unclogs the pores and reduces inflammation. It is also somewhat effective at killing bacteria.

Hydroxy Acids

Salicylic acid is a beta hydroxy acid. Glycolic acid is an alpha hydroxy acid, as are lactic acid, citric acid, and many others. Hydroxy acids are compounds that are both alcohols and acids at the same time. Hydroxy acids are used as chemical peeling agents. Alpha hydroxy acids can make the skin more sensitive to ultraviolet light by removing the skin's protective outer layers.

Some alpha hydroxy acids:

- citric acid
- lactic acid
- ammonium glycolate
- alpha-hydroxycaprylic acid

- alpha-hydroxyethanoic acid
- alpha-hydroxyoctanoic acid
- glycolic acid (sometimes called fruit acid or sugar cane extract)
- malic acid

Salicylic Acid

Chemical Formula
$C_6H_4(OH)CO_2H$

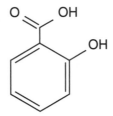

Synonyms
2-hydroxybenzoic acid

Description
White odorless crystals.

Uses
Salicylic acid is used to treat acne, warts, dandruff, psoriasis, and similar conditions. In the treatment of acne, it slows the shedding of skin cells in hair follicles, so they do not clog the pores and cause pimples. It also has a *keratolytic* effect—it causes dead skin cells to slough off—which removes the top layer of skin and clears existing pore clogs.

In treatments for warts, a stronger solution is used. Not only does this soften the wart so it can be rubbed off, but the irritation also stimulates the immune system to attack the underlying cause of warts, human papillomavirus.

Salicylic acid reacts with acetic acid to produce acetylsalicylic acid the active ingredient in aspirin. It also reacts with methanol to form methyl salicylate, more commonly known as oil of wintergreen.

Salicylic acid is common in foods such as broccoli, peppers, curry, cucumbers, and raisins, among many others.

Salicylic acid reduces inflammation, including inflammation of the arteries. In arteries it can work to prevent hardening and narrowing.

Sulfur

Chemical Formula
S

Description
Yellow crystals or powder.

Uses
Sulfur is used in acne medications to treat inflamed lesions (pimples). It can cause whiteheads and blackheads (comedones) if used by itself, so it is usually combined with salicylic acid, benzoyl peroxide, or resorcinol, which eliminates comedones.

Resorcinol

Chemical Formula
$C_6H_4(OH)_2$

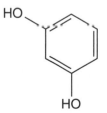

Synonyms
M-dihydroxybenzene • 1,3-benzenediol • 3-hydroxyphenol

Description
White or off-white needle-shaped water-soluble crystals.

Uses
As an acne treatment, resorcinol has a *keratolytic* effect—it causes dead skin cells to slough off—which removes the top layer of skin and unclogs pores. It is often used with sulfur, to prevent the whiteheads and blackheads that may be a side effect when sulfur is used to treat inflamed pimples.

Like salicylic acid, it is also used to treat warts, psoriasis, and other skin conditions.

Hydrogen Peroxide

Chemical Formula
H_2O_2

$$
\begin{array}{c}
H \\
| \\
O - O \\
| \\
H
\end{array}
$$

Description
Clear, colorless liquid.

Uses
Hydrogen peroxide is used as a topical antiseptic in dilute solutions, and as a water purifier in stronger solutions.

It is also famous as a hair bleach.

Hydrogen peroxide breaks down into water and oxygen. A liter of 3 percent hydrogen peroxide will generate 10 liters of oxygen when a catalyst is used to facilitate the breakdown. Catalysts can be metals such as iron, copper, or silver, or organics such as the blood enzyme catalase (like hemoglobin, catalase contains iron, which catalyzes the reaction).

Catalase is an important enzyme in cells because hydrogen peroxide is a by-product of metabolism and can poison the cell unless it is decomposed quickly. Hydrogen peroxide is also produced by cells in the immune system, and catalase removes the excess.

The 3 percent hydrogen peroxide you get at the drugstore is often protected from decomposing by the addition of sodium silicate, magnesium sulfate, or tin compounds. These stabilizers lock up the iron, copper, and other transition metals that can act as catalysts.

Sodium Bicarbonate

Chemical Formula
$NaHCO_3$

Synonyms
Bicarbonate of soda • baking soda

Description
White powder.

Uses
Sodium bicarbonate is used as a leavening in breads, as a stomach antacid, as a buffering agent to adjust the acidity or alkalinity of a product, as a mild abrasive in toothpaste, and as an odor absorber.

Sodium bicarbonate reacts with acids to release carbon dioxide gas.

Hydroquinone

Chemical Formula

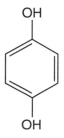

Description

Off-white powder or white needlelike crystals.

Hydroquinone inhibits melanin production when applied to the skin. The effect is reversible by exposure to ultraviolet light.

Uses

Hydroquinone in a 2 percent solution is used in many skin-lightening creams and gels to remove freckles, age spots, and other hyper-pigmented areas of the skin.

Since sunlight reverses the effect, a sunscreen is usually mixed into the preparation.

Antibiotics

Triclosan

See entry, page 25.

Triclocarban

See entry, page 25.

Hexachlorophene

See entry, page 26.

Pain Relievers

Potassium Nitrate

Chemical Formula
KNO_3

Synonyms
Saltpeter

Description
White crystals.

Uses
Potassium nitrate is best known as the oxidizing agent in old-fashioned "black powder" gunpowder, which is 75 percent potassium nitrate by weight. The other ingredients are 15 percent charcoal and 10 percent sulfur.

But potassium nitrate is also used in toothpastes that are formulated to make teeth less sensitive to pain. As gums recede and the tooth root dentin becomes exposed, teeth can become hypersensitive to hot or cold foods. Potassium nitrate interferes with the transmission of pain signals in the nerves of the teeth.

Potassium nitrate is also found in pills for backache and joint pain. It makes a decent plant fertilizer, providing nitrogen and potassium but no phosphorus. As an oxidizer, it is an ingredient in stump removers that hastens the decay of tree stumps. And it is used as a preservative in some salted meats; like nitrites, it helps to preserve the color of the meat.

Benzocaine

Chemical Formula

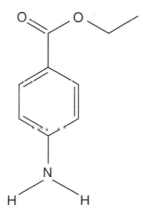

Synonyms
Ethyl p-aminobenzoate • ethyl PABA • anesthesin

Description
White crystalline powder.

Uses
Benzocaine is a topical anesthetic. It numbs any area to which it is applied. It is widely used in first-aid creams and sunburn remedies.

 **Chemistry Lesson**

Benzocaine is an ester, a compound made from the organic acid PABA (para-amino benzoic acid) and the alcohol ethanol.

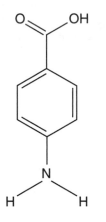

Para-amino benzoic acid

Other esters of PABA have similar anesthetic properties.

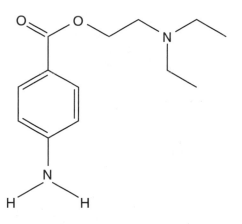

Procaine (novocaine)

Dentists use procaine (also called novocaine) to numb teeth and gums before dental work.

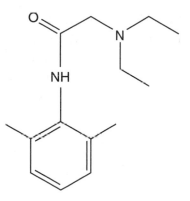

Lidocaine (xylocaine)

Another topical anesthetic, similar to benzocaine, is lidocaine, which is used to relieve the pain of shingles (herpes zoster) infections. Lidocaine is called an amide anesthetic, because it is not an ester (the alcohol is replaced by an amide, the nitrogen group). Amide anesthetics are metabolized by the liver, and are less prone to cause allergic reactions. If an anesthetic has the letter *i* in the prefix (lidocaine, prilocaine, bupivacaine), it is an amide anesthetic.

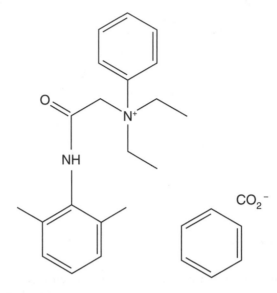

Denatonium benzoate

A small change to lidocaine (adding a benzyl group) makes the molecule denatonium benzoate, the bitterest tasting substance known. It is used to *denature* alcohol—to make it unfit for drinking. Specially denatured alcohol 40, or SD-40, is ethanol denatured (made unfit for drinking) by a tiny amount denatonium benzoate.

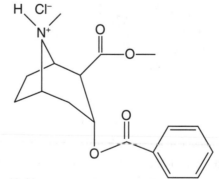

Cocaine hydrochloride

You can see a resemblance between benzocaine, procaine, and the compound that gave Coca-Cola its first name. Cocaine also has a numbing effect, in addition to its effects as an addictive central nervous system stimulant.

Some other anesthetics with similar structures are prilocaine, tetracaine, ropivacaine, bupivacaine, chloroprocaine, and mepivacaine:

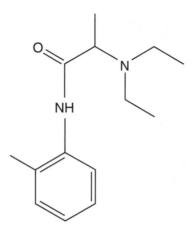

Prilocaine

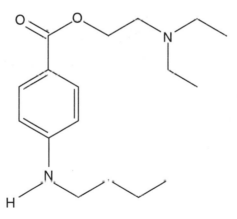

Tetracaine

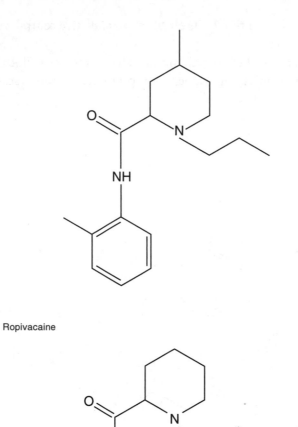

Ropivacaine

Bupivicaine

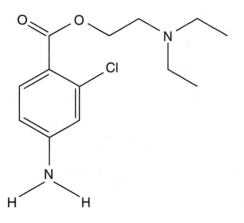

Chloroprocaine

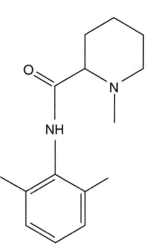

Mepivacaine

Tramadol

Chemical Formula

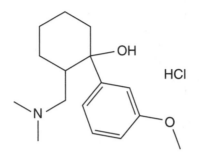

Synonyms
(+/-)cis-2-((dimethylamino)methyl)-1-(3-methoxyphenyl)-cyclo-hexanol hydrochloride

Description
White, odorless, bitter crystalline powder.

Uses
Tramadol is a pain reliever (analgesic). Its action is similar to opioid narcotics such as codeine and morphine, but it does not depress breathing the way the others can, and less often leads to abuse and addiction.

 ## Chemistry Lesson

Tramadol is an alkaloid, with an amine group (where the nitrogen atom is), which puts it in a group of bitter plant chemicals that often have potent biological activity.

Alkaloids range from the belladonna alkaloids, such as atropine and scopalomine—which are used as poisons, cold remedies, and "truth serums"—to dextromethorphan, a cough suppressant (antitussive). But the most widely known alkaloids are the opiates, such as morphine, heroin, fentanyl, oxycodone, and methadone. These act on receptors in the brain that are normally activated by small proteins (peptides) called endomorphins or endorphins.

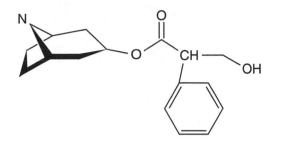

Atropine

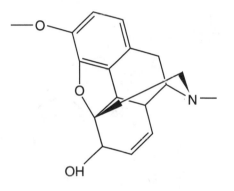

Codeine

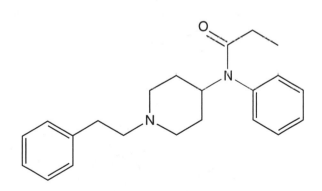

Fentanyl

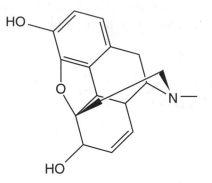

Morphine

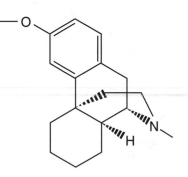

Heroin

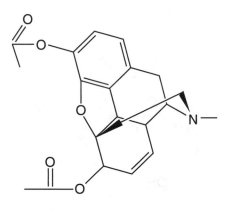

Dextromethorphan

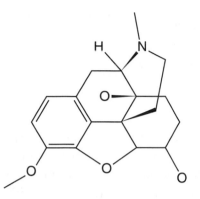

Oxycodone (OxyContin)

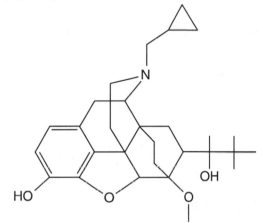

Buprenorphine

Acetylsalicylic Acid

Chemical Formula
$C_6H_4(OCOCH_3)CO_2H$

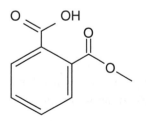

Synonyms
Aspirin • 2-acetoxybenzoic acid

Description
White odorless crystals.

Uses
Acetylsalicylic acid is more commonly known as aspirin. It is used as a pain reliever, fever reducer, and anti-inflammatory.

Acetylsalicylic acid breaks down into salicylic acid 20 minutes after entering the bloodstream. It is the salicylic acid that is responsible for the beneficial effects of aspirin. Salicylic acid itself is too caustic to be taken orally.

Acetylsalicylic acid has an anticlotting effect in the blood.

Acetaminophen

Chemical Formula
$C_8H_8NO_2$

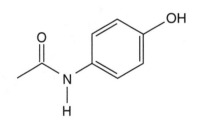

Synonyms
Tylenol • paracetamol • N-acetyl-para-aminophenol • para-acetyl-amino-phenol

Description
Bitter white powder.

Uses
Acetaminophen is a pain reliever similar to aspirin, but it does not have aspirin's anti-inflammatory properties—or its undesirable effects

on the stomach lining. It also lacks aspirin's anticoagulatory effects. Acetaminophen is often combined with opiates such as codeine and dihydrocodeine to form a more potent painkiller.

Unlike aspirin and other cyclooxygenase inhibitors that work on the COX-1 and COX-2 enzymes, acetaminophen works on the COX-3 enzyme, which is present in the spinal column and brain. This helps it to avoid shutting down prostaglandin function elsewhere in the body, which is why it has no anti-inflammatory effects and does not affect blood platelets or the stomach lining.

Ibuprofen

Chemical Formula
$C_{13}H_{18}O_2$

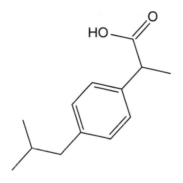

Synonyms
Advil

Description
White powder

Uses
Like aspirin, ibuprofen is a nonsteroidal anti-inflammatory drug. It is a cyclooxygenase inhibitor that interferes with COX-1 and COX-2 forms of that enzyme. Its effects on COX-2 give it fever-reducing (antipyretic), analgesic (pain relief), and anti-inflammatory functions.

Its effects on COX-1 give it several undesirable effects: it is an anticoagulant, and it irritates the stomach lining.

Ibuprofen is used to relieve fever and pain, and symptoms of arthritis and menstrual cramping. It may also reduce the dizziness associated with standing up quickly (called orthostatic hypotension), and some studies have shown that it may have beneficial effects for patients suffering from Alzheimer's disease and Parkinson's disease.

Naproxen

Chemical Formula
$C_{14}H_{14}O_3$

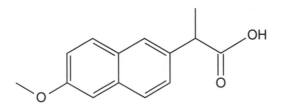

Synonyms
Aleve • naproxen sodium

Description
White powder.

Uses
Like aspirin, naproxen is a nonsteroidal anti-inflammatory drug. It is a cyclooxygenase inhibitor that interferes with COX-1 and COX-2 forms of that enzyme. Its effects on COX-2 give it fever-reducing (antipyretic), analgesic (pain relief), and anti-inflammatory functions. Its effects on COX-1 give it several undesirable effects: it is an anticoagulant, and it irritates the stomach lining.

Naproxen is used to relieve fever, pain, and symptoms of arthritis, gout, bursitis, and menstrual cramping.

Naproxen has been found to increase the risk of heart attack and stroke by 50 percent.

Allantoin

Chemical Formula
$C_4H_6N_4O_3$

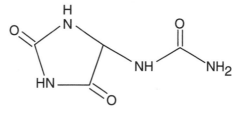

Synonyms
Glyoxyldiureide • comfrey root extract

Description
White, odorless, tasteless crystals or powder.

Uses
Allantoin relieves the skin irritation caused by soaps and detergents, acids, and alkalies in oral- and skin-care products.

Some studies claim that it promotes wound healing and tissue formation, but regulatory agencies do not credit these claims.

Menthol

See entry, page 59.

Methyl Salicylate, Ethyl Salicylate, Glycol Salicylate

Chemical Formulas
$C_8H_8O_3$, $C_9H_{10}NO_3$, and $C_9H_{10}O_4$

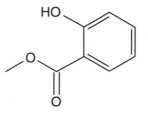

Methyl salicylate

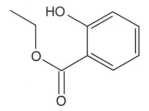

Ethyl salicylate

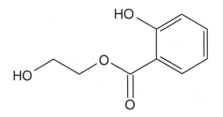

Glycol salicylate

Synonyms
Oil of wintergreen • salicylic acid • methyl ester • methyl sweet birch oil • betula oil

Description
Reddish or yellow liquid.

Uses
Wintergreen is used as a flavoring in foods, beverages, drugs, and candies. It is also used as a perfume in root beer, and as an ultraviolet light absorber in cosmetics.

It serves as a pain reliever in liniments and ointments. It is a *rubefacient*, meaning that it can dilate blood vessels.

The most widely used salicylate is aspirin.

Camphor

Chemical Formula
$C_{10}H_{16}O$

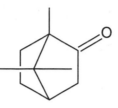

Synonyms
2-camphanone • 1,7,7-trimethylbicyclo[2.2.1]-2-heptanone

Description
White crystals.

Uses
Camphor is a rubefacient—it relieves mild pain and itching, and creates inflammation and redness when rubbed into the skin. Much like menthol, it has a cooling effect when applied to the skin.

Camphor is used in acne medications, cough remedies, ear drops, and other medications where its ability to soothe the skin helps it to counter the effects of other ingredients that might otherwise be irritants.

Methyl Nicotinate and Benzyl Nicotinate

Chemical Formula
$C_7H_7NO_2$ and $C_{13}H_{11}NO_2$

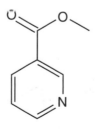

Methyl nicotinate

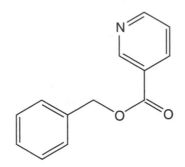

Benzyl nicotinate

Synonyms
Niacin methyl ester • nicometh • 3-carbomethoxypyridine • methyl 3-pyridinecarboxylate • 3-pyridinecarboxylic acid • methyl ester

Description
White crystalline powder and yellow liquid.

Uses
The B vitamin niacin is also known as nicotinic acid. The body converts various forms of the vitamin into forms it can use.

The methyl ester and benzyl ester forms can be used as a rubefacient (a vasodilator that opens up capillaries, which as a side effect makes the skin redden). It also works to reduce plasma cholesterol.

Niacin is recommended to alleviate pellagra, a disease caused by a deficiency of this vitamin.

Capsaicin

Chemical Formula
$C_{18}H_{27}NO_3$

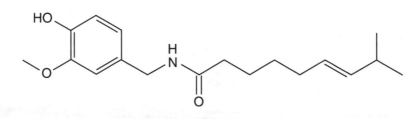

Synonyms
8-methyl-N-vanillyl-6-nonenamide • capsicum oleoresin

Description
Colorless, odorless waxy crystals.

Uses
Capsaicin is what makes chili peppers hot. It is an irritant for mammals, but not for birds. This may be because birds spread the seeds better than mammals. It causes a burning sensation in any mammalian tissue with which it comes in contact.

Capsaicin is a nonpolar molecule; it dissolves in fats and oils, not in water. This is why water does not take away the burning sensation, but whole milk or other fat-containing liquids or foods will.

As an ingredient in medicines, capsaicin is used to relieve pain from arthritis, muscle aches, and sprains. It is a rubefacient, meaning it dilates blood vessels. The heat effect overwhelms nerves, causing a localized numbing sensation.

Capsaicin is also used in pepper spray.

Bleaching Agents

17

Sometimes rather than adding color to a product, it is necessary to take color away. We bleach our clothes, our hair, and sometimes even our food. Most often chemicals react with colorful compounds to make them colorless through a process called *oxidation*.

Sodium Hypochlorite

Chemical Formula
NaOCl

Synonyms
Chlorine bleach

Description
Sodium hypochlorite is usually sold in solution in water, where it makes a greenish-yellow liquid. (It is too hygroscopic—it absorbs water from the air—to be used conveniently in solid form.) Household bleaches usually contain sodium hypochlorite in a 3 percent to 6 percent solution. Some sodium hydroxide (lye) is added to keep the pH high to avoid decomposition. If the solution is made more acidic, sodium hypochlorite will dissociate, producing chlorine gas and oxygen.

Sodium hypochlorite is made by bubbling chlorine gas through a solution of sodium hydroxide. In the environment, it breaks down into water, oxygen, and table salt.

Uses

Sodium hypochlorite is the main ingredient in laundry bleach. Despite the fact that it is commonly referred to as chlorine bleach, in normal use there is no chlorine gas involved in the action of bleaching or disinfecting.

Sodium hypochlorite is one of the best disinfectants known, capable of killing bacteria, yeasts, fungus, spores, and even viruses. Because it is an excellent disinfectant as well as a bleaching agent, it is used in many household cleaners. Sodium hypochlorite is also used to disinfect water supplies and swimming pools (although calcium hypochlorite in powder or pellet form is often used as a substitute, due to the convenience of its solid form).

Focus: Bleach

We bleach our clothes. We bleach our hair. We bleach our teeth. We bleach our skin. We bleach our food. We use bleaches to disinfect and deodorize.

Some bleaches smell awful. Some, like lemon juice and sunshine, are refreshing. Here are a few things you should know about bleach.

Color and Bleach

Colored substances contain molecules with chromophores, areas of the molecule that have double bonds between carbon atoms or oxygen atoms. A good example is beta-carotene, and that section goes into more detail on how molecules become colored. Bleaches attack these chromophores in one of two ways.

First, *oxidizing bleaches* such as sodium hypochlorite break the molecules at the double bond. This results in either a shorter molecule that does not absorb visible light, or a molecule whose chromophore is either shorter or nonexistent. A shorter chromophore will absorb light of a shorter wavelength than visible light (such as ultraviolet light), and so does not appear colored.

Second, *reducing bleaches* such as lemon juice (in combination with sunlight) or sulfur dioxide convert the double bonds in the chromophore into single bonds, eliminating its ability to absorb visible light. Sometimes the reaction is reversible, where oxygen in the air reacts with the molecule to repair the chromophore, and the stain returns.

Bleaching Clothing

Laundry bleaches fall into two categories. The first is what are called *chlorine bleaches*. The second is *oxygen bleaches*.

While pure chlorine gas will certainly bleach colors, laundry bleaches use sodium hypochlorite or calcium hypochlorite, which works by releasing oxygen, not chlorine. The chlorine remains in solution, either as sodium chloride (table salt), or calcium chloride. These bleaches are made by bubbling chlorine gas through a solution of sodium hydroxide (lye) or calcium hydroxide (quicklime).

If the bleach is mixed with an acid, it can release poisonous chlorine gas. To prevent this from happening, commercial bleaches leave extra alkalies in the solution to keep the pH very high (pH 12). This small amount of extra lye in the solution, along with the caustic nature of the hypochlorite itself, is what eats away the cloth if undiluted bleach gets spilled on the clothing.

Another chlorine bleach in common use is sodium dichloroisocyanurate.

Oxygen bleaches also work by releasing oxygen. Hydrogen peroxide is the active ingredient, either as itself or as a product of reacting another ingredient with water to release hydrogen peroxide.

Oxygen bleaches such as sodium carbonate peroxide (also called sodium percarbonate), sodium peroxide, or sodium perborate are made by reacting molecules with hydrogen peroxide. When the result is added to water, the hydrogen peroxide is released.

Borax also works by releasing hydrogen peroxide into the water.

   Most oxygen bleaches work best in hot water. Additives such as tetra acetyl ethylene diamine allow the hydrogen peroxide to work in warm water (50°C).

Bleaching Hair

Ultraviolet light from the sun is the most common hair-bleaching agent. Lemon juice is sometimes added to speed up the process of reducing the double bonds in hair pigments to single bonds.

   However, the most famous hair bleach is hydrogen peroxide. Unlike sunlight and lemon juice, peroxide is an oxidizing bleach, and its effects are less easily undone.

   The calcium hypochlorite or sodium dichloroisocyanurate used to disinfect swimming pools also bleaches hair, although contrary to popular belief it does not turn the hair green. It simply allows the green copper sulfate from the *water* to show up in the hair. The copper sulfate comes from the reaction of the copper pipes in the plumbing to the sulfuric acid used to neutralize the alkalies in the chlorination chemicals.

Bleaching Teeth

Dental bleaches are an ingredient in whitening toothpastes and in whitening gels or strips applied to the teeth. Whitening toothpastes most often use sodium carbonate peroxide. In gels and strips, carbamide peroxide is used, often with tetra acetyl ethylene diamine as a bleach activator. All of these products owe their bleaching action to the hydrogen peroxide that is liberated during application.

Bleaching Skin

Skin lighteners, freckle and age spot removers, and other remedies for hyperpigmentation are not actually bleaches like the products listed so far. The active ingredient is hydroquinone, which inhibits melanin formation when applied to the skin. Since the effect is easily reversed by exposure to sunlight or ultraviolet light, a sunscreen is usually included in the formula.

Bleaching Food

Wheat flour typically becomes white by means of normal oxidation in air during a few weeks of storage. To speed up the process, manufacturers use benzoyl peroxide as a bleaching agent. Sulfur dioxide is a reducing bleaching agent that is used to preserve dried fruits.

Disinfecting

Oxidizing bleaches kill microbes by reacting with cell membranes and cell proteins. The most widely used is sodium hypochlorite for household and hospital uses, and calcium hypochlorite for drinking water and swimming pool disinfecting.

Calcium Hypochlorite

Chemical Formula
CaOCl

Synonyms
Chlorine tablets

Description
White powder or tablets.

It is made by bubbling chlorine gas through a solution of calcium hydroxide.

Uses
Calcium hypochlorite is the main ingredient in swimming pool chlorine tablets.

Calcium hypochlorite is one of the best disinfectants known; it kills bacteria, yeasts, fungus, spores, and even viruses. It is more commonly used to disinfect water supplies and swimming pools than its close cousin sodium hypochlorite (household bleach) because it can be sold as a solid (it does not attract moisture from the air and clump up as sodium hypochlorite powder does).

Hydrogen Peroxide

See entry, page 168.

Benzoyl Peroxide

See entry, page 163.

Borax

Chemical Formula
$Na_2B_4O_7$

Synonyms
Sodium borate decahydrate • sodium tetraborate decahydrate • sodium biborate • sodium pyroborate

Description
White powder.

Uses
Borax is used in laundry detergents and bleaches. It releases hydrogen peroxide when it reacts with water. Hydrogen peroxide acts as a bleach, and its action is aided by the alkaline solution also produced by the reaction.

Borax is a good buffer, helping to stabilize the acidity or alkalinity of a solution.

The boron (along with the oxygen and salt) in a borax solution helps to disinfect by killing bacteria and fungi.

Sodium Perborate

Chemical Formula
$NaBO_3$

Description
White powder.

Uses

Sodium perborate is used in laundry detergents and bleaches. It releases more hydrogen peroxide than borax when it reacts with water. Hydrogen peroxide acts as a bleach, and its action is aided by the alkaline solution that is also produced by the reaction.

Sodium Carbonate Peroxide

Chemical Formula
$2Na_2CO_3 \cdot 3H_2O_2$

Synonyms

Peroxy sodium carbonate • sodium percarbonate

Description

White granules.

Uses

Sodium carbonate peroxide breaks down into sodium carbonate and hydrogen peroxide. The hydrogen peroxide acts as a bleach and as an antimicrobial agent. The high alkalinity of the sodium carbonate boosts the bleaching effect of hydrogen peroxide.

Sodium Dichloroisocyanurate

Chemical Formula

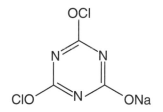

Synonyms

Sodium chlorocyanurate • 1,3-dichloro-1,3,5-triazine-2,4,6(1H,3H, 5H)-trione sodium salt • SDIC

Description

White powder with a strong chlorine odor.

Uses

Sodium dichloroisocyanurate is used as a disinfectant in swimming pools and as a bleaching agent in household cleansers.

Hydroquinone

See entry, page 169.

Surfactants

18

To remove fats, oils, and grease from our clothes, our hair, our bodies, and our dishes, we use products known as surfactants. These contain ingredients that make oil and water mix, forming tiny droplets out of oil slicks, so the droplets can be washed away in the rinse water.

Ammonium Lauryl Sulfate

Chemical Formula

$CH_3(CH_2)_{10}CH_2OSO_3NH_4$

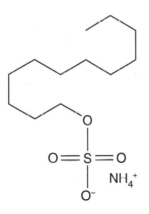

Synonyms
Dodecyl ammonium sulfate

Description
Light yellow viscous liquid.

Uses
Ammonium lauryl sulfate is an *anionic surfactant*. This means it lowers the surface tension of water, making the water spread more easily. Surfactants are also called *wetting agents*—in plain terms, they make water wetter.

Ammonium lauryl sulfate is added to products as a foaming agent and as a detergent. Notice in the structural formula that one end of the molecule is a long chain of carbon and hydrogen, while the other end is a salt of sulfuric acid and ammonia. The long chain is hydrophobic, and the salt is hydrophilic, making this a good detergent and surfactant.

Ammonium lauryl sulfate is used in many shampoos, toothpastes, and skin cleansers. Unlike soap, it can be used in hard water.

When ammonium lauryl sulfate is reacted with ethylene oxide, the result is the larger molecule ammonium laureth sulfate. This molecule has the same detergent and surfactant qualities, but it is larger; consequently it does not penetrate the skin and hair as easily. The term *laureth* is actually a contraction of *lauryl ether*. The full name is ammonium lauryl ether sulfate.

Sodium lauryl sulfate is the same compound and has the same uses, but in this case the ammonium group has been replaced with a sodium atom.

Focus: Shampoo

 Television would have you believe that shampoo will change your love life, make you suave and sophisticated, or fill you with awe at how shiny your hair has become.

Shampoo

The purpose of a shampoo is to clean hair. But the shampoo must not clean too well, or all of the protective oils in the hair will be stripped out. It must also not make the hair smell bad, despite the bad smells of the detergents it is made of.

To sell well, the shampoo must look good, must feel thick or creamy in the hands, and must produce a nice-feeling lather. It must smell good, and it must not be too expensive. Other selling points might be the currently popular herbal extracts, or amino acids from exotic protein sources such as silk or the milk of pygmy goats.

Detergents

The most common ingredient in shampoos is also the most common detergent in use in other products: a class of surfactants known as straight-chain alkyl benzene sulfonates. Examples are ammonium lauryl sulfate, its sodium relative, and the slightly larger but related molecule ammonium lauryl ether sulfate (sometimes abbreviated as ammonium laureth sulfate).

These detergents work best in water that has little calcium and magnesium, as these elements bind to the detergent and make an insoluble scum. Tetrasodium EDTA often is used to sequester the calcium and magnesium from the detergent, while keeping them soluble enough to rinse away without scum.

Cocamide DEA (or MEA or TEA) is used as a foaming agent, to make lather. The other surfactants generate a certain amount of suds, but this foaming agent is added to get the amount just right. In addition to its foam-stabilizing effects, it is also a viscosity booster—it's thick.

Another foam stabilizing detergent is PEG-5 cocamide, which is also a surfactant and emulsifier.

The detergent cocamidopropyl betaine is added because it is milder on the skin than the benzine sulfonates, which means that adding it to the mix reduces the amount of the harsher detergents needed. It is thicker than the other ingredients, so it can be added to give the mix the right viscosity. It has antistatic properties; it helps keep the hair from generating an electric charge when it's dry and jumping to plastic combs and brushes. It is also a humectant, attracting moisture from the air, thus keeping hair from drying out. And it has antibiotic properties that can prevent the shampoo from spoiling.

The surfactant ammonium xylenesulfonate is used as both a thickener and a *hydrotrope*, a compound that makes it easier for water to dissolve other molecules. It helps keep other ingredients in solution, including some of the odd substances that are added for marketing effect, such as perfumes. Glycerol stearate is another emulsifier used for this purpose.

Special Effects

The wax glycol distearate is added to make shampoos opaque and pearlescent. It has tiny flakes that mix well with surfactants, and stay in solution. They also add shear-thinning qualities, making liquid hand soaps pump out of the bottle more easily.

Sodium chloride (table salt) is used to thicken the mixture if the main surfactants are sodium lauryl sulfates. If the surfactants are ammonium-based, then ammonium chloride is used instead. Salt can make the shampoo harsh, which can sting the eyes, so more expensive thickeners are used to keep the salt levels low.

Modified cellulose-based thickeners are often used, along with the surfactant-based thickeners already mentioned.

Glycerin is added as a humectant (draws moisture from the air), as is propylene glycol, which is also a preservative.

There are many additives in shampoos and conditioners that appear to be there mainly for marketing purposes. Honey, various herb extracts, and other compounds might add to the fragrance, but they are unlikely to have any other effects in the small concentrations used. Amino acids can act as conditioners, but the source of the amino acid is not important. Silk amino acids are essentially no different from soy amino acids.

Preservatives

Two widely used preservatives, DMDM hydantoin and imidazolidinyl urea, are ingredients used in many shampoos to prevent fungal and bacterial spoilage. They release formaldehyde to kill germs.

Other broad-spectrum biocides are isothiazolinone and the closely related methylisothiazolinone and methylchloroisothiazolinone.

Sodium benzoate is another preservative used in shampoos. It kills bacteria, fungi, and yeasts, and works well in acidic mixtures.

Another commonly used bactericide is 2-bromo-2-nitropropane-1,3-diol.

pH Balance

The surface of a strand of hair is covered with overlapping sheets, somewhat like the scales on a fish or the shingles on a house. This surface is called the cuticle. Alkaline solutions raise these scales, so they stand up. This makes the hair shafts stick together, which in turn makes the hair look and feel rougher and duller.

Most shampoos are made slightly acidic, to keep the cuticle smooth and lying flat on the hair shaft. Ingredients like citric acid are added to acidify the shampoo.

As shampoo is applied to the hair and scalp, it can become less acidic as the acids mix with alkaline water or dirt. A compound that releases more acidifying ions when the acidity gets low or absorbs acid when the acidity gets too high is called a buffer.

A typical buffering agent used in shampoo is sodium citrate. Since the goal is to keep the shampoo slightly acid, the term "pH balanced" is actually a misnomer. You actually want the balance to be tipped slightly to the acidic side.

Conditioners

Conditioners are compounds added to keep the hair cuticle smooth and slippery. Silicone oils such as dimethicone and cyclomethicone are used to make the hair shiny and slippery. Humectants (moisturizers) like panthenol help keep the cuticle moist so that the scales do not stand up. Long-chain fatty alcohols such as cetyl alcohol, oleyl alcohol, and stearyl alcohol lubricate the hair. One end of the molecule binds to the hair, leaving the slippery fatty end on the outside to rub against other strands of hair or a comb.

Quaternary ammonium compounds are cationic surfactants that bind well to anionic surfaces like the protein in hair. The ammonium end sticks to the hair, leaving the long fatty end of the molecule to act as a lubricant. They are slightly conductive, so they reduce the buildup of static electricity. *Quats*, as they are sometimes called, include compounds like stearalkonium chloride, disteardimonium chloride, quaternium-5, or quaternium-18, polyquaternium-10 and they are all similar in form and function to cetrimonium chloride. These compounds are also widely used as fabric softeners, for all of the same reasons they make good hair conditioners. They are also used to thicken the shampoo.

The emollient isopropyl palmitate is used as a skin softener, moisturizer, and antistatic agent.

Sodium Lauryl Sarcosinate

Chemical Formula
$CH_3(CH_2)_{10}CH_2C_3H_6NNaO_2$

Description
Light yellow viscous liquid.

Uses
Sodium lauryl sarcosinate is very similar to the lauryl sulfate class of detergents and surfactants. The sulfate group is replaced with the amino acid sarcosinic acid, and the ammonium group is replaced with a sodium atom. The result is a detergent that is milder on the skin and oral membranes, and can be used in toothpastes without causing irritation of the gums.

Lauryl Glucoside

Chemical Formula

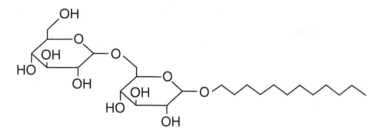

Synonyms
Lauryl diglucoside

Description
Viscous liquid.

Lauryl glucoside (lauryl diglucoside) is a surfactant and detergent made from coconut oil (the "lauryl" part) and sugar (the "glucose" part). Such alkyl glycosides biodegrade quickly, and tend to be gentle to the skin, and they work in hard water.

Uses
Lauryl diglucoside is used in shampoos as a detergent and as a thickening agent.

Cocamidopropyl Betaine

Chemical Formula

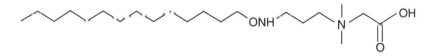

Synonyms
Inner salt • coco betaine

Description
Pale yellow transparent liquid.

Uses
Cocamidopropyl betaine is an *amphoteric* detergent, a detergent that can act as an acid or a base. It does not irritate the skin or mucous membranes. It is used to thicken shampoos, and to reduce the irritation that would result if only more irritating detergents were used. It has antibiotic effects, and is used in personal sanitary products. It also has antistatic properties, making it an effective conditioning agent in shampoos.

Sodium Stearate

Chemical Formula
$CH_3(CH_2)_{16}COONa$

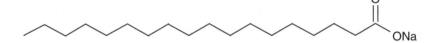

Synonyms
Soap

Description
Sodium stearate is one of the main compounds in common soap. To make soap, you start with beef fat. If you treat beef fat with steam you get tallow, a mixture of fats, one of which is glyceryl tristearate:

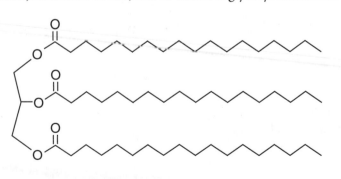

a triglyceride containing three stearic acid molecules attached to a glycerin molecule.

When you boil glyceryl tristearate in lye (sodium hydroxide), you get sodium stearate and glycerin. When you remove the glycerin, you get soap.

The sodium end of the molecule attracts water. The long hydrocarbon chain at the other end attracts oils and fats.

Uses

Soap works by helping to break fat and oil droplets into small pieces. The pieces are coated with the soap, with the hydrocarbon chains attached to the fat, leaving the sodium ends dangling in the water. The oils are now completely surrounded by water, instead of being attached to skin or clothing, and so they rinse away easily.

Focus: Soap

We like to be clean. Clean feels good. It smells good. Clean means fewer microbes are around to hurt us. Clean clothes feel good. Clean dishes make food safer and more attractive.

For thousands of years, soap was the last word in clean.

Soap

The first soaps were probably the saps of plants such as *Chlorogalum pomeridianum*, the roots of which can be crushed in water to form a lather. Other plants, such as soaphark (*Quillaja saponaria*), snapberry (*Sapindus mukorossi*), and soapwort (*Saponaria officinalis*) also contain the same main ingredient, a compound called saponin, which forms the foamy lather. (Saponin can also be used in fishing; a toxin, it is introduced into streams to stupefy fish and make them easy to catch.)

Later, people learned that fats would react with alkalies in the ashes left over from a fire to produce saponified compounds such as sodium stearate and the closely related potassium stearate.

Today, soaps are made from fats and oils that react with lye (sodium hydroxide). Solid fats like coconut oil, palm oil, tallow (rendered beef fat), or lard (rendered pork fat), are used to form bars of soap that stay hard and resist dissolving in the water left in the soap dish.

Oils such as olive oil, soybean oil, or canola oil make softer soaps. Castile soap is any soap that is made primarily of olive oil. This type of soap is known for being mild and soft.

As warm liquid fats react with lye and begin to saponify, they thicken like pudding. At this point dyes and perfumes are often added. The hardening liquid is then poured into molds, where it continues to react by generating heat. After a day, the bars can be cut and wrapped, but the saponification process continues for a few weeks, until all of the lye has reacted with the oils.

Soaps are often "superfatted," so after all of the lye has reacted with the fats, there are still fats left over. This is important for two reasons. First, the resulting soap is easier to cut and feels smoother on the skin. Second, the extra fats ensure that all of the lye reacts, so no lye is left to irritate the skin.

The saponification process results in about 75 percent soap and 25 percent glycerin. In homemade soaps, the glycerin is left in, as it acts as an emollient (skin softener) and creates a nice feel. In commercial soaps, the glycerin is often removed and sold separately, sometimes showing up in skin moisturizers that remedy soap's skin-drying effects.

Commercial bar soaps contain sodium tallowate, sodium cocoate, sodium palmate, and similar ingredients, all of which are the results of reacting solid fats—tallow, coconut oil, and palm kernel oil, respectively—with lye.

To these ingredients, they add fatty acids such as coconut acid and palm acid (the fats in coconut oil and palm kernel oil).

These extra fats ensure that the lye is completely reacted and that the soap has a good feel.

Polyethylene glycols such as PEG-6 methyl ether may be added as either surfactants, detergents, emulsifiers (to make the dyes and perfumes blend evenly), or thickeners.

Glycerin is added as an emollient and texture enhancer. Sorbitol is another emollient that is often used along with glycerin because it makes the soap more transparent. Titanium dioxide is added to make the soap opaque.

Pentasodium pentetate, tetrasodium etidronate, and tetrasodium EDTA are added as water softeners and to protect the dyes and perfumes from the effects of metal ions in the mixtures. These compounds lock up calcium and magnesium in the water, preventing them from reacting with the soap to form insoluble soap scum.

Detergent Bars

Not all bars that lather contain just soap. Many feature the same detergents that you find in shampoo as well.

In addition to the soaps and fatty acids, some bars contain cocamidopropyl betaine, a mild amphoteric detergent that is added to control irritation without decreasing suds or cleaning power, and benzine sulfonate detergents such as sodium dodecylbenzinesulfonate. Other detergents, such as sodium isethionate and sodium cocoyl isethionate, are also common.

Preservatives

BHT (butylated hydroxytoluene) is sometimes added as an antioxidant preservative to keep the oils from going rancid.

Antimicrobials

Antibacterial soaps usually contain triclosan or triclocarban as the active antibacterial ingredient.

Sodium Dodecylbenzenesulfonate

Chemical Formula

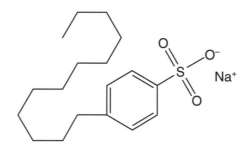

Synonyms
Sodium 4-dodecylbenzenesulfonate

Description
White or light yellow flakes.

Sodium dodecylbenzenesulfonate is a straight-chain benzene sulfonate, a type of detergent.

Uses
Straight-chain benzene sulfonates were invented as replacements for branched-chain benzene sulfonates, which were the first detergents but which could not be easily broken down by microbes in streams, rivers, or sewage treatment plants.

These detergents are in use in many products, from laundry detergents to detergent soap bars. They are the most common type of detergent in use.

Sodium Isethionate

Chemical Formula

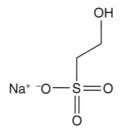

Synonyms
Sodium 2-hydroxyethanesulphonate • sodium cocoyl isethionate

Description
White solid or flakes.

Uses
Sodium isethionate is an amphoteric detergent used in detergent bar soaps. It makes a dense lather in addition to the lather made by the soap. It is nondrying and mild on the skin. It works equally well in soft or hard water. It is also an antistatic agent in shampoos.

Sodium cocoyl isethionate is a related amphoteric detergent used in mild bath soaps, toothpastes, and baby soaps.

Focus: Detergents

No matter how much fun it is to squish our toes in the mud, most people love to be clean. We want our clothes to be fresh, our dishes to be spotless, and our cars to be shiny. We continue to invent new ways to make things clean.

Detergents

Detergents have molecules with one side that prefers water (hydrophilic), and another side that prefers oils and fats (hydrophobic). The hydrophilic side attaches to water molecules, and the hydrophobic side attaches to oil molecules. This action allows the oil droplets to break up into smaller droplets surrounded by water. These smaller droplets, no longer stuck to the material to be cleaned, are washed away.

Surfactants

Detergents and soaps are surfactants, which is short for "surface-active agent."

Surfactants have a hydrophilic side of the molecule that attaches to water, and a hydrophobic side of the molecule that avoids water. In the absence of oils, the hydrophobic side sticks out of the surface of the water drop. There is no longer any water at the surface to form a strong surface tension, so the water no longer beads up, but spreads. The hydrophobic end of the molecule is also free to attach to grease, fat, or oil on the surface, which aids in the spreading.

Emulsifiers

Some detergents and surfactants are used as emulsifying agents. An emulsifier keeps oil droplets and water droplets from joining together, so a thick mixture of oil and water will not separate. Examples of emulsions are mayonnaise, butter, cream, homogenized milk, and salad dressings.

Soap

Beef fat reacting to alkaline wood ashes led to the creation of the earliest soap, and it has been the cleaning product of choice for millennia. Soap is made from a fatty acid that is reacted with an alkali. The acid end of the fatty acid reacts with the alkali to form a salt that is water soluble. The other end is the fatty end, which repels water and is attracted to fats and oils. The process of making soap is called saponification.

Types of Detergents

German scientists created the first detergents during the shortages of World War II. These were called branched-chain alkyl benzene sulfonates. Like soap, they could take hard minerals out of water, leaving it soft. As with soap, the minerals formed a scum, familiar to anyone who has seen a bathtub ring.

Microbes could not break down branch-chain detergents, so they left foam in river water. They were replaced by straight-chain alkyl benzene sulfonates, such as sodium dodecylbenzene-sulfonate and sodium xylenesulfonate.

Straight-chain detergents don't work in hard water. Phosphates were added to detergents to soften the water, but phosphates are excellent fertilizer for algae in rivers and oceans. The algae blooms deplete the oxygen in the water, which in turn kills fish. Phosphates were replaced with other water softeners such as sodium carbonate and EDTA.

Later, surface-acting polyglucosides were created. These sugar-based detergents are easily broken down by microbes, leaving no traces in the environment. They consist of a pair of glucose molecules, with hydrocarbon side chains attached to act as the hydrophobic ends. They are milder than soaps, and they work in hard water.

Another type of detergent is a group called the pyrrolidones. These are complex molecules that dissolve in both water and organic solvents.

Additives

Some laundry detergents contain "optical brighteners." These are fluorescent dyes that glow blue-white in ultraviolet light. The blue-white color makes yellowed fabrics appear white.

Laundry detergent may also contain polyethylene glycol, a polymer that prevents dirt from redepositing on the clothes. This function used to be the job of phosphates. Another polymer used for this purpose is carboxy methyl cellulose, which is derived from natural cellulose but is very soluble in water.

Yet another ingredient in laundry detergents is diethyl ester dimethyl ammonium chloride (DEEDMAC). It is a fabric softener. It is a cationic surfactant that is rapidly biodegradable. It works by reducing the friction between fibers, and between fibers and the skin. Cationic surfactants are those where the hydrophilic part (in this case the ammonium chloride) is positively charged, and is attracted to substrates that are negatively charged, such as proteins and many synthetic fabrics. Hair conditioners use this trick also. You can think of hair conditioner as fabric softener for your head.

A cationic surfactant will often have an ammonium group attached to a halogen, as in the ammonium chloride mentioned above. Anionic surfactants, such as soap, often have a sodium, potassium, or ammonium group, as in sodium stearate.

Nonionic surfactants like polyethylene glycol esters (PEG) are used as mild cleansers, or to add viscosity to mixtures such as shampoo.

Amphoteric surfactants are those that are an acid and a base at the same time (like water is). Cocamidopropyl betaine, for example, is used in shampoos to stabilize foam and thicken the mixture.

Some examples of detergents and surfactants are:

- ammonium lauryl sulfate
- lauryl glucoside

Classes of detergents:

- Alkyl benzene sulfonates (ABS). Branched-chain anionic surfactants. Slow to biodegrade. Seldom used.
- Linear alkyl benzene sulfonates (LAS). Straight-chain anionic surfactants. Somewhat slow to biodegrade. Most common surfactants in use.
- Alkyl phenoxy polyethoxy ethanols (alcohol ethoxylates). Also called nonyl phenoxy ethoxylate, or nonyl phonol. Slow to biodegrade. Nonionic surfactant. Used in dry detergents.
- Diethanolamine and triethanolamine. Commonly used to neutralize acids in shampoos, to reduce irritation (pH-balanced shampoos). Slow to biodegrade.

- Alkyl ammonium chloride (quaternium-15). Acts as a surfactant, disinfectant, and deodorant.
- Alkyl glycosides. Quick to biodegrade. Made from oils and sugar.

Detergent additives:

- Mono ethanol amine (MEA). A solvent used to dissolve other laundry detergent ingredients. It also lowers the freezing point of liquid laundry products to allow them to be transported in cold weather.
- Sodium carbonate peroxide. Used as a bleach. It breaks down into sodium carbonate and hydrogen peroxide, which does the actual bleaching.
- Sodium sulfate. Used to dilute powdered detergents.

Xylenesulfonates

See entry, page 138.

Foam Stabilizers

19

Foams are formed when surfactants mix with air instead of with oils or fats, and adding one of those substances generally makes the foams break down. For instance, beating egg whites into a foam is much harder to do if grease or oil is added to the egg white mixture. Likewise, if you want a thick lather on your hair, you will have to use more shampoo than is needed to remove the dirt and oil.

Since we want the texture of products like shaving cream to stay stable, and since shampoo advertisers like to pretend that unnecessary extra lather is an important selling point, foam stabilizers are helpful in preventing foams from breaking down.

Cocamide MEA
Cocamide DEA
Cocamide TEA

Chemical Formula

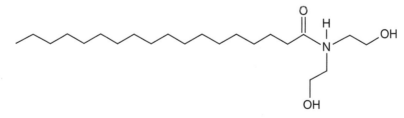

Cocamide DEA

Synonyms
Coconut fatty acid monoethanolamide • coconut fatty acid diethanolamide • coconut fatty acid triethanolamide • N-coco alkyl derivatives

Description
Viscous clear to amber liquid, or solid flakes.

These ingredients are made from fatty acids in coconut oils, reacted with diethanolamine, or its mono- or triethanolamine relatives.

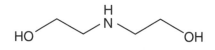

Diethanolamine

Uses
Cocamide ethanolamines are used as foaming agents in shampoos and bath products and as emulsifying agents in cosmetics.

Tetrasodium Pyrophosphate

See entry, page 46.

Conditioners

20

Conditioners are surfactants that neutralize the electrical charge on the surface of the hair, and smooth down protein scales on the hair shafts. These effects make the hair easier to style and less prone to static electricity.

Conditioners can be made from oily surfactants or fatty surfactants, or a mixture of both. The more solid fatty conditioners can glue together split ends and damaged hair. The more liquid oily conditioners smooth the hair and then rinse out more effectively.

Cetyl Alcohol

See entry, page 57.

Cetrimonium Chloride

Chemical Formula

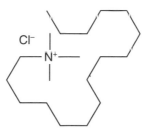

Synonyms

1-hexadecanaminium • cetyltrimethylammonium chloride • C16-alkyltrimethylammonium chloride

Description

Clear liquid.

Uses

Cetrimonium chloride is used in hair conditioners, fabric softeners, and antistatic agents for hair and fibers. It makes fabrics and hair less prone to static electricity buildup by making them slightly conductive.

Silicones

Chemical Formula

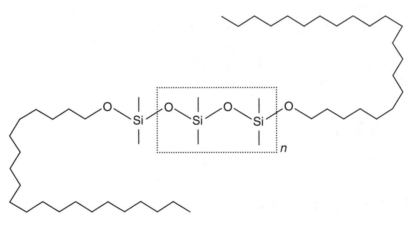

Dimethicone

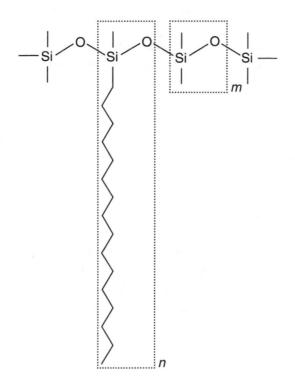

Cetyl dimethicone

Synonyms
Polydimethylsiloxane (PDMS) • dimethicone • cyclomethicone • cetyl dimethicone • cyclopentasiloxane • silicone oil

Description
Slippery liquid.

Silicones are a large group of compounds that include large polymers containing silicon. Depending on the formula and the degree of polymerization and cross-linking of the polymers, they may be slippery liquids, waxes, or rubbers.

Uses

Silicones are used as emollients (skin softeners), as lubricants, as thickeners, and as volatile liquids that make coatings feel smooth but evaporate without leaving a greasy residue.

Highly cross-linked silicone films are used in cosmetics to form coatings that absorb sebum (skin oils) and prevent shine.

Cyclopentasiloxane is a low-viscosity, volatile liquid that is used as a carrier. It lubricates, and prevents hairsprays from being sticky to the touch. It evaporates completely, leaving no residue.

Dimethicone is another name for polydimethylsiloxane and is used to impart a soft velvety feel to hair or skin products. It is also used as an emulsifier for water-in-oil emulsions.

Trimethylsiloxysilicate is a film-forming resin that is used to keep hand lotions and sunscreens from washing off.

Cetearyl methicone is a polysiloxane wax. It replaces petrolatum in such products as hand lotions to give them a nongreasy feel.

Panthenol

See entry, page 126.

Propellants

21

Propellants are gases or liquids that quickly expand into gases to carry a substance (often a glue, as in the case of hairspray, but sometimes a foam, as in whipped cream) out of its container.

Nitrous Oxide

Chemical Formula
N_2O

$$N = N = O$$
$$N \equiv N - O$$

Bonds resonate between single/triple and double

Synonyms
Dinitrogen oxide • dinitrogen monoxide

Description
Colorless, nonflammable gas with a sweet odor.

Uses
Nitrous oxide is used as a foaming agent and propellant in whipped cream. It dissolves easily in fats under pressure, and comes out of solu-

tion when the pressure is reduced, much like the carbon dioxide in a can of soda.

Nitrous oxide dissolves in the fats that sheath the nerve cells, and produces numbing and mild intoxication. It is the "laughing gas" dentists use to make patients less aware of pain.

Many gases dissolve in fats and make good propellants. However, most are flammable or toxic, or they react with the fats. Other possible propellants, such as the propane used in hairsprays or in Freon, also cause intoxication when they dissolve in the fats around nerve cells. These substances are not used, since their flammability, safety, cost, or taste makes them less desirable than nitrous oxide for spray cans of whipping cream.

Isobutane

Chemical Formula
C_4H_{10}

Synonyms
Butane

Description
Colorless, odorless gas.

Uses
Isobutane is used in cigarette lighters and camp stoves as a fuel. It is easily liquefied under pressure, and the liquid becomes a gas immediately when the pressure is released. It is also used as a propellant in hairsprays and spray breath fresheners.

Chemistry Lesson

Isobutane is a compound in a class of chemicals called alkanes. Alkanes are chains of carbon atoms where each carbon atom has as many hydrogen atoms attached as possible. This means that all of the bonds between carbon atoms are single bonds (no double bonds). Such a molecule is said to be saturated.

The simplest alkane has only one carbon atom. It is called methane:

Methane, CH₄

It appears here with all of the hydrogens showing. In pictures of the structural formulas in organic chemistry, carbon atoms and hydrogen atoms typically aren't shown because the picture would just be too crowded. A carbon atom is implied whenever a line ends or whenever one line joins another. Hydrogens are assumed to connect to any carbon that has a free bond. (Carbon can form four bonds, so if only three are showing, the other is attached to a hydrogen.)

Ethane, C₂H₆

Using this convention, ethane is just a line. There is a carbon at each end, and each carbon has three bonds left, so there are six hydrogens in the molecule.

Propane, C₃H₈

Propane is a bent line. There is a carbon at each end, and one in the middle, at the bend. Each carbon at an end has three bonds, and the carbon in the middle has only two bonds left, so we have eight hydrogens in the molecule.

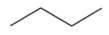

Butane, C_4H_{10}

Butane has four carbons. With four carbons, we suddenly have two different ways the carbons can link up. They can be all in a row, like the molecule shown above, or one carbon can be in the middle, bonding to three carbons and a hydrogen.

Isobutane, C_4H_{10}

An alkane with all the carbons in a row is called butane, and the form with one carbon in the middle is known as isobutane. The *iso* is short for *isomer*, which means a molecule that has the same atoms arranged in a different way.

Pentane, C_5H_{12}

When there are five carbons, there are three different ways to arrange them. A pentane is an alkane molecule where the carbons are all in a row.

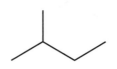

2-methylbutano, C_5H_{12}

When molecules start to get complicated like this, they must be named carefully, according to some rules. One rule is to look for the longest unbranched alkane in the molecule. In this molecule, it is butane (four carbons). Next, describe the branch. In this case, it is methane (one carbon). Then describe where the branch is attached. In this case, it is attached to the second carbon in butane. The name is thus 2-methylbutane.

2,2-dimethylpropane, C_5H_{12}

The other way five carbon atoms can be arranged in an alkane is to attach two of them to the middle carbon atom in propane. The molecule above has two methanes and a propane, and both methanes are attached to the second carbon in the propane. Thus it is called 2,2-dimethylpropane.

Up until pentane, all of these alkanes were gases. Pentane is a liquid. The longer the chain of carbons gets, the harder it is for one of the molecules to escape into the air.

Hexane, C_6H_{14}

Hexane is next. There are many ways to put six carbons together; there are only two forms shown here. The first is simply the carbons all in a row.

Cyclohexane, C_6H_{12}

Another way to put six carbons together is to attach them in a ring. The result is not the same as hexane, because the two hydrogens at the end of hexane are missing. The ring form is called cyclohexane. While three carbons could have formed a three-sided ring, the bonds would be very strained, and the molecule would be unstable. Likewise, four and five carbon rings can form, but they are also less stable, and break down into the other forms. But with six carbons, the molecule is quite stable and stays in a ring easily.

Heptane

The simple chain made of seven carbons is called heptane.

Octane

When eight carbons occur in a chain, it is called octane. A mixture of liquid alkanes we call gasoline burns in our automobiles. If the mixture has a lot of lightweight molecules that evaporate easily, it can ignite too readily in the engine, causing premature ignition, or "knocks and pings." If the gasoline has more of the longer molecules, it burns more slowly, and only ignites when the spark plug fires. These gasolines are called high-octane fuels.

Alkanes keep going up in size. When they get up to $C_{18}H_{38}$ they become solids. The familiar white solid paraffin, which is commonly used for making candles, is made up of solid alkanes. Paraffin is not really a wax, as waxes are made up of more complicated molecules.

Dimethyl Ether

Chemical Formula

Synonyms
1,2-dimethoxyethane

Description
Colorless, flammable gas with an odor of ether.

Uses
Dimethyl ether is used as a propellant in aerosols. It is also a solvent, a fuel used in welding, and a refrigerant. In high concentrations, it has an anesthetic effect.

Polymers and Glues

Glues are often polymers, long-chained molecules that bind things together either by reacting with them or by trapping them in a tangle.

Vinyl Acetate

Chemical Formula

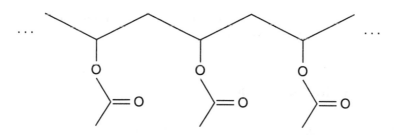

Synonyms
Poly(vinyl acetate) • PVA • vinyl acetate/crotonates/vinyl neode-canoate copolymer

Description
White powder.

Uses

Polyvinyl acetate is an ingredient in white glue. It is a copolymer with vinyl alcohol in latex paints.

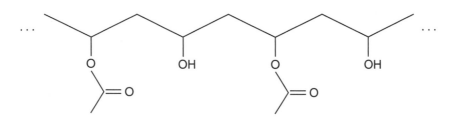

Copolymer of vinyl acetate and vinyl alcohol

This molecule is a copolymer with polymethyl methacrylate (PMMA) in acrylic latex paints, where the hydrophobic PMMA is surrounded by hydrophilic polyvinyl acetate molecules. Such a suspension of a hydrophobic polymer wrapped in a hydrophilic polymer is called a latex.

A copolymer is a polymer made up of two or more different building blocks, called monomers.

 **Chemistry Lesson**

Many common plastics are made from simple building blocks called vinyl monomers. These are little molecules that contain carbon double bonds. The simplest one is ethylene:

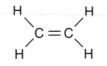

Ethylene molecules can join together into immensely long chains, converting the double bond into a single bond as they join to become polyethylene.

When the propylene molecule polymerizes, the result is polypropylene.

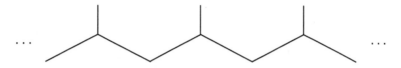

When the vinyl chloride molecule polymerizes, polyvinylchloride (PVC) is the result.

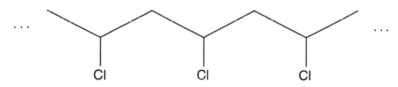

When the styrene molecule polymerizes, the result is polystyrene—Styrofoam.

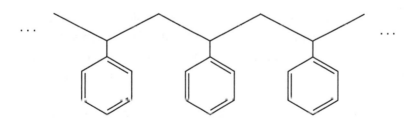

When the methyl methacrylate molecule polymerizes, it is polymethyl methacrylate—Plexiglas.

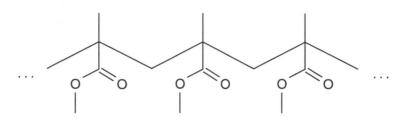

When the tetrafluoroethylene molecule polymerizes, it's poly-tetrafluoroethylene, more commonly known as Teflon.

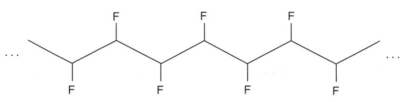

Focus: Hairspray

 It's just a simple little spray can with a simple task—to keep hair in place. So why does it contain so many different ingredients?

Hairspray is formulated to hold hair in place and keep it shiny, without flaking off, without failing, even in humid conditions. Yet it must retain the ability to be washed out of the hair easily for at least forty-eight hours, and it must not clog the spray can's nozzle. Complex polymers are needed to perform all of these tasks well. The basic building blocks of these polymers are the same ones found in acrylic paints and white glue. But they are put together in a different way.

The two main polymers used in hairspray are vinyl acetate/crotonates/vinyl neodecanoate copolymer (a form of vinyl acetate) and octylacrylamide/acrylates/butylaminoethyl methacrylate copolymer (a form of methacrylate). These polymers are carried in a base of water and alcohol (usually denatured), and the liquefied gas dimethyl ether, which acts as the propellant. The dimethyl ether boils away as a gas when the spray head is pushed down, propelling the rest of the ingredients out in a fine mist.

The emulsifier aminomethyl propanol serves several purposes in hairspray. It acts as a buffering agent, controlling the acidity of the mixture to make it neutral ("pH balanced"). It also helps keep the polymers mixed with the water and alcohol, and controls the water solubility of the final mist, giving it the needed humidity resistance. It also helps to form the polymers into a gel.

Sodium benzoate is used as a preservative, although it also functions as a corrosion inhibitor.

Cyclopentasiloxane is a volatile silicone used to make the film water-repellent, and to eliminate tackiness. It is a thickener; it acts as a lubricant and gives the resulting coating a silkier feel.

Sodium PCA is a moisturizing agent; it draws moisture from the air and holds it.

Some sprays include vitamins such as tocopherols (vitamin E) or panthenol, which is metabolized in the skin to become pantothenic acid, a B vitamin. Since hair does not metabolize ("It's dead, Jim"), these sprays perform the functions of antioxidants (tocopherols). In other words, they add shine and moisture (panthenol) rather than perform their normal vitamin roles. Moisture helps prevent damage during combing.

Hydrolyzed soy proteins are also sometimes added to hairspray. These are more commonly known as soy sauce and MSG (monosodium glutamate), an amino acid.

Butylene glycol is sometimes used as a humectant (moisturizer) and preservative if the spray contains food items such as vitamins and proteins. It also helps products to retain their scents.

Vinyl Alcohol

Chemical Formula

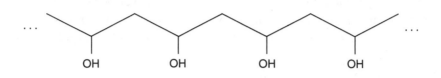

Synonyms
PVA

Description
White powder.

Uses
Polyvinyl alcohol is a main ingredient in latex paints, hairsprays, shampoos, and glues. It forms polymers and copolymers with other monomers, such as vinyl acetate and methyl methacrylate

When the polymers are cross linked using borax, you get the children's toy Slime.

Methacrylate

Chemical Formula

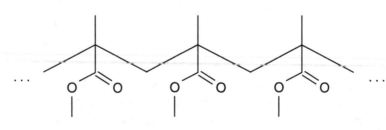

Synonyms

Polymethyl methacrylate (PMMA) • octylacrylamide/acrylates/butyl-aminoethyl methacrylate copolymer • Plexiglas

Description

Clear solid.

Methacrylates and acrylates are a large group of polymers that together form acrylic plastics used in many common household products.

Uses

Acrylics are used in floor polish, hairsprays, latex paints, and glues as well as plastic items and packaging.

Silicones

See entry, page 220.

Abrasives and Dental Additives

So what are all those things in my toothpaste? How can it polish, whiten, prevent cavities, prevent plaque, prevent gum disease, and freshen my breath all at the same time?

Hydrated Silica

Chemical Formula

$SiO_2 \cdot nH_2O$

$SiO_2 = 1$, $H_2O = 1$: H_2SiO_3

$SiO_2 = 2$, $H_2O = 1$: $H_2Si_2O_5$

$SiO_2 = 2$, $H_2O = 3$: $H_2Si_2O_7$

$SiO_2 = 3$, $H_2O = 2$: $H_2Si_2O_8$

$SiO_2 = 3$, $H_2O = 4$: $H_2Si_2O_{10}$

$SiO_2 = 4$, $H_2O = 1$: $H_2Si_2O_2$

$SiO_2 = 4$, $H_2O = 2$: H_2SiO_2 (also known as $Si(OH)_4$)

Synonyms
Silicic acid • silica gel • amorphous silicon dioxide

Description

A transparent colloid (gel).

Uses

Hydrated silica is the abrasive used in gel toothpastes, or in the clear portion of striped toothpastes. It is often used as a secondary abrasive in opaque toothpastes as well.

When dried in an oven, hydrated silica loses its water and becomes a desiccant (a substance that attracts water from the air). You find little packets of silica gel crystals in containers whose contents would be damaged by condensing moisture, such as vitamin bottles, consumer electronics, pepperoni, or leather products.

Silica gel can be made by reacting an acid with sodium silicate, which is sold in drug stores as "water glass" or "egg keep," and is used to paint eggs to seal them from air and prevent spoilage. Drying the resulting gel will get the desiccant, or it can be used wet in toothpastes.

You can find sodium silicate in the colorful Magic Rocks seen in gift shops at museums. The dry form is mixed with salts of various metals. When you drop them in water, the sodium is replaced by the metal. The resulting metallic silicate is not soluble in water, and it takes on a color characteristic of the metal (e.g., copper is blue). The metallic silicate is also a gel, so it expands and grows into colorful stalagmites in the water.

Focus: Toothpaste

The quality of toothpaste seems to improve every day. We have anticavity toothpaste, extra-whitening toothpaste, toothpaste with mouthwash, toothpaste for sensitive teeth, toothpaste with stripes, clear toothpaste, and even liver-flavored toothpaste for dogs.

Modern toothpaste has to do many things. It must have abrasives to scour off bacterial films. It must have fluorides to harden the teeth against decay. It must have a strong enough pleasant flavor to hide the bad tastes of decaying bits of previous meals, as well as the awful taste of some of the other ingredients, such as detergents and phosphates.

Toothpaste must have thickeners to help it squeeze out of the tube and stay on the toothbrush. It must have detergents to remove fatty films, water softeners to make the detergents work better, and sweeteners (preferably non-nutritive so as not encourage bacteria).

Toothpaste Ingredients

The most recognized toothpaste ingredient is probably the class of compounds known as fluorides. Stannous fluoride was the first to be used in toothpaste because, unlike sodium fluoride, it did not lose its effectiveness when combined with the abrasive most common at the time, calcium phosphate. Later, sodium mono-fluorophosphate came into popular use because it too could be used with the common abrasives.

When hydrated silica became the abrasive of choice, sodium fluoride could be used, and it has become the most widely used fluoride in contemporary toothpaste.

Hydrated silica is the transparent abrasive used in gel tooth-pastes and in the clear parts of striped toothpaste. It has come into common use in white opaque toothpastes as well, because of its compatibility with sodium fluoride.

Fluorides work better in combination with surfactants, which help the remineralization process. The most common are the lauryl sulfates, such as sodium lauryl sulfate or ammonium lauryl sulfate.

Surfactants (detergents) also help clean the teeth; they provide a foam that helps to carry away debris. Moreover, lauryl sulfates have significant antibacterial properties, and they can penetrate and dissolve plaque.

Lauryl sulfates can irritate oral membranes, and so a similar detergent, lauryl sarcosinate, often replaces some or all of the lauryl sulfate. Allantoin is sometimes added to relieve irritation caused by detergents, alkalies, and acids.

The sequestering agent tetrasodium pyrophosphate (TSPP) removes calcium and magnesium from the saliva, so they can't deposit on teeth as insoluble deposits called tartar (calcified plaque). In this respect it acts as a water-softening agent. However, it won't remove tartar that already exists.

TSPP is slightly alkaline and has a bitter taste, requiring additional flavorings to mask it. Also, additional detergents must be added to keep it in solution. All of these factors can irritate oral membranes and cause sensitivity.

Polymers such as the acrylic PVM/MA copolymer are added to prevent bacteria from breaking down pyrophosphates. Other long polymers used are polyethylene glycol (PEG) in various weights (PEG-6, PEG-8, PEG-40, etc.), and polypropylene glycol (PPG).

Sodium bicarbonate (baking soda) is added for taste and "mouth feel." It combines with acids to release carbon dioxide gas, adding to the foam produced by brushing. It is a mild abrasive. It may reduce the numbers of acid-loving bacteria in the mouth, although this effect lasts only as long as the mouth stays alkaline.

Sodium carbonate peroxide is added to "peroxide" toothpaste as a whitener. It breaks down into sodium carbonate (washing soda) and hydrogen peroxide. The hydrogen peroxide bleaches the teeth and kills germs.

Sweeteners such as sodium saccharin are added for taste. Other flavors are usually strong essential oils in the mint family.

The antibacterial agent triclosan is added to kill plaque-forming microbes.

Various types of gum are used to thicken the paste. They also help retain moisture, so the toothpaste does not dry out if the top is not replaced.

Titanium dioxide is used to make pastes opaque and white.

Stannous Fluoride

Chemical Formula
SnF_2

Synonyms
Tin fluoride

Description
White crystals.

Uses
Stannous fluoride is used in toothpastes and dental rinses to protect tooth enamel from attack by bacteria—cavities (also known as dental caries). It was the first fluoride used for that purpose, in the toothpaste Crest.

The active part of the molecule is the fluoride ion, which is why two other fluorine-containing compounds, sodium fluoride and sodium monofluorophosphate, are also used.

Stannous fluoride can be used with abrasives that contain calcium, which prevents sodium fluoride from being effective. Sodium monofluorophosphate was developed to avoid infringing on the Crest patent.

Fluorides work in two ways. They reduce the ability of bacteria to make acids, and they remineralize the areas of the tooth that have been attacked by acids from bacteria.

Sodium Fluoride

Chemical Formula
NaF

Description
White crystals.

Uses

Sodium fluoride is used in toothpastes and dental rinses to protect tooth enamel from attack by bacteria—cavities (also known as dental caries).

The active part of the molecule is the fluoride ion, which is why two other fluorine-containing compounds, stannous fluoride (tin fluoride) and sodium monofluorophosphate, are also used.

Fluorides work in two ways. They reduce the ability of bacteria to make acids, and they remineralize the areas of the tooth that have been attacked by acids from bacteria.

Sodium Monofluorophosphate

Chemical Formula
Na_2PO_3F

Synonyms
MFP

Description
White crystals.

Uses

Sodium monofluorophosphate is used in toothpastes to protect tooth enamel from attack by bacteria—cavities (also known as dental caries). It was developed to avoid infringing on the Crest patent for stannous fluoride.

The active part of the molecule is the fluoride ion, which is why two other fluorine-containing compounds, sodium fluoride and stannous fluoride, are also used.

Like stannous fluoride, sodium monofluorophosphate can be used with abrasives that contain calcium, which prevents sodium fluoride from being effective.

Fluorides work in two ways. They reduce the ability of bacteria to make acids, and they remineralize the areas of the tooth that have been attacked by acids from bacteria.

Index